For you to trick my old teacher! Love ya.
me

THE
UNITED STATES
OF
TRIVIA

THE
UNITED STATES
OF
TRIVIA

WILLIAM MacKAY & MAUREEN SLATTERY

★ ☆ ★

FALL RIVER PRESS

New York

FALL RIVER PRESS

New York

An Imprint of Sterling Publishing
387 Park Avenue South
New York, NY 10016

Jacket design by David Ter-Avanesyan

ISBN 978-1-4351-5300-4

For information about custom editions, special sales, and premium and
corporate purchases, please contact Sterling Special Sales at 800-805-5489
or specialsales@sterlingpublishing.com.

Manufactured in the United States of America

2 4 6 8 10 9 7 5 3 1

www.sterlingpublishing.com

To Ellen Pease, a dear friend and
a superlative sister

*   *   *

The authors wish to thank Rick Campbell,
Sallye Leventhal, Mike Katz, Heather Rodino,
and, of course, our editor Chris Barsanti.

THE UNITED STATES OF TRIVIA

1 Q:
How did a nineteen-year-old Clovis, New Mexico, teenager change what we know about prehistory in the Americas?

2 Q:
Hundreds of years before the arrival of Columbus, the Anasazi, or Ancient Ones, established their own thriving culture in the Four Corners region of the American Southwest. What was the most spectacular accomplishment of these ancestral Puebloans?

3 Q:
What happened to the Anasazi?

4 Q:
Which American city boasts the longest continuous habitation by Europeans?

5 Q:
What is the oldest state capital city in the United States?

1. Boston, Massachusetts
2. Frankfort, Kentucky
3. Santa Fe, New Mexico
4. Richmond, Virginia
5. Providence, Rhode Island

THE UNITED STATES OF TRIVIA

1 A: When former Boy Scout James Ridgley Whiteman found stone tools associated with mammoth bones in 1929, he knew that he had made a significant discovery and wrote to the Smithsonian Institute about his find. Later radiocarbon tests established that these "Clovis points" had been made approximately 13,500 years ago, pushing back the date of humans in the New World by thousands of years. Subsequent archaeological digs in Chile, Brazil, and Pennsylvania have extended the timeline even further back.

2 A: The Anasazi's masterfully planned and executed cliff dwellings are among the architectural wonders of the New World.

3 A: No one knows for certain. For decades archaeologists and historians have been debating the causes of the sudden collapse of the Anasazi empire in the late thirteenth century. Theories have ranged from environmental stress caused by rapid climatic changes to disease, warfare, and even cannibalism.

4 A: St. Augustine, Florida. Founded in 1565 by Spaniard Pedro Menéndez, the settlement was established forty-two years before the English colonized Jamestown, Virginia.

5 A:
3. New Mexico only became a state in 1912, but its capital city was first settled more than three centuries earlier, in 1609.

6 Q:

According to legend, one early Spanish conquistador was on a personal mission when he landed in what would later become a U.S. state. Name the explorer, the state, and his supposed secret purpose.

7 Q:

Where was the Lost Colony and how did it get lost?

8 Q:

What clues were found at the site about the missing English settlers?

6 A: That Ponce de León landed in present-day Florida in 1513 and gave it its name is beyond dispute. What appears to be apocryphal, however, is that he was searching for a mythical Fountain of Youth. In any case, he didn't find it: Just eight years later, at age forty-seven, he was killed by a poison arrow.

7 A: In 1587, English settlers reestablished a colony on Roanoke Island, although the island had been the site of an Indian massacre just the previous year. When Governor John White returned from an extended resupply trip to England in 1590, he found the island deserted, dismantled, and perhaps plundered. Theories abound, but no one knows for sure what happened to the 117 colonists.

8 A: White's crew found the word "CROATOAN" carved onto a fence post and "CRO" cut into a nearby tree. Because all the houses and fortifications had been dismantled and not simply abandoned, White concluded that their departure had not been hurried and that for some reason, the Roanoke contingent had relocated to Croatoan Island (now Hatteras Island). Unfortunately, White's sailors refused to pursue the lead because a massive storm was brewing. In recent years, a DNA project has been undertaken to determine whether Lost Colony survivors might have intermarried with local Native Americans.

9 Q:

When was tobacco first grown for smoking and chewing purposes?

10 Q:

When did the Pilgrims land on Plymouth Rock?

11 Q:

In 1620, colonists signed a concise 200-word declaration that has rightly come to be regarded as a major document in American history. Identify this landmark agreement.

12 Q:

There were eighteen adult women among the *Mayflower* Pilgrims; how many survived until the first Thanksgiving in 1621?

9 A: The natives of the Americas used tobacco as far back as 2,000 years ago. Columbus, an apparent convert, brought the plant back to Spain, where its use (to the chagrin of many) spread throughout Europe.

10 A: The short answer is that they didn't: In 1620 they first made landfall in the New World at what is now Provincetown. The dubious story of a Plymouth Rock landing was first told by Thomas Faunce, a ninety-five-year-old who told the tale more than a century after the pilgrim's arrival.

11 A: The Mayflower Compact. By signing the covenant on November 11, forty-one Plymouth settlers agreed to establish a "civil body politic," a government in their new home. Many historians view this document as the beginning of constitutional government in America. Others, obviously more cynical, dismiss it as no more than a temporary fix designed to avert a possible mutiny.

12 A: Four. None of them died during the two-month journey, but once they arrived at Provincetown, the women were confined to the ship while the men built houses on shore. The boat's damp and dirty conditions led to the high mortality rate.

13 Q:

In what year did Pocahontas marry Captain John Smith?

14 Q:

What story about Pocahontas and Captain John Smith has been told and retold; recreated in plays, movies, and books; and is still controversial among scholars?

15 Q:

What does the state name "Oklahoma" mean in the Choctaw language?

13 A: She never did. This Native American woman, whose real name was Matoaka, converted to Christianity and was baptized as Rebecca. In 1614, she married Englishman John Rolfe. Two years later, she and her husband sailed to England, where she was presented at the court of James I. Before she could return to America, she contracted smallpox and died.

14 A: According to this well-known story, Pocahontas saved the Jamestown military leader from Native American execution. In December 1607, Smith had been taken prisoner and was about to be clubbed to death by her father Chief Powhatan and his tribesmen when Pocahontas intervened. Some historians argue that the colonist's story was totally concocted or had "grown better" over time. Though he was a prolific author, Smith never recounted the episode himself until nearly nine years after the event, and his fullest account was not published until more than a decade later. In any case, its effectiveness in middle-school presentations cannot be disputed.

15 A: The name "Oklahoma" comes from the Choctaw words "okla" meaning "people," and "humma" meaning "red," so the state's name literally means "red people."

16 Q:
What was the first book published in what would become the United States and why is it still making headlines?

17 Q:
When did Americans start drinking tea?

16 A: The book that Stephen Day published as *The Whole Booke of Psalmes Faithfully Translated into English Metre* was first distributed in 1640, just twenty years after the Pilgrims arrived. Now known universally as *The Bay Psalm Book*, this small, 148-page book has become an invaluable rarity. (Of the original 1,700 copies, only eleven have survived.) In November 2013, a fine copy sold for $14.2 million, a record for a printed book.

17 A: Governor Peter Stuyvesant brought tea to Dutch New Amsterdam in 1650. It quickly became so popular that English visitors to the small settlement now renamed New York consumed more tea than the entire country of England.

Identify the British Parliamentary Acts leading to the American Revolution.

18 Q: At the end of the French and Indian War in 1763, Parliament ended the colonies' exemption from revenue-raising taxes to help pay for the Crown's large war debt. Strict enforcement of the new policy hampered colonial smuggling operations.

19 Q: This 1765 law required government watermarks on all paper used for newspapers and legal documents. Unfortunately for Parliament, the people most affected by the tax were newspaper printers, and their headlines encouraged public opposition.

20 Q: After the repeal of the Stamp Act, another series of revenue-raising measures was passed beginning in 1767. Duties were imposed on seventy-two consumer goods in the colonies, including wine, fruit, chinaware, lead, and paint.

21 Q: After the Boston Tea Party, Parliament imposed a series of retaliatory measures. One of the 1774 laws was nicknamed the "Murder Act" by George Washington because it allowed British officials accused of crimes and offenses against Americans to be tried in England.

18 A: The Sugar Act.

19 A: The Stamp Act.

20 A: Townshend Acts, named after then Chancellor Charles Townshend.

21 A: Coercive or Intolerable Acts.

———

22 Q:

Which of the following acts was *not* part of the Coercive Acts passed by the British Parliament?

1. Quartering Act
2. Stamp Act
3. Tea Act
4. Boston Port Act
5. Adminstrative of Justice Acts

23 Q:

What is the Mason–Dixon Line?

24 Q:

Who was Patrick Henry? What is his famous quote?

25 Q:

There are reports that Henry didn't write the speech that he delivered so effectively. If he didn't, who did?

26 Q:

For Americans, "the shot heard round the world" most frequently refers to the beginning of the Revolutionary War and the battles of Lexington and Concord. How was this association made?

22 A:
2, Stamp Act, and 3, Tea Act.

23 A: In 1763, Charles Mason and Jeremiah Dixon were commissioned by the heirs of William Penn and Lord Baltimore to settle an old border dispute between Pennsylvania and Maryland. What began as a latitude boundary line between two states became known as the dividing line between free states and slave states, and it is now regarded as the boundary between the North and the South.

24 A: Henry was a prominent Virginia attorney, planter, slave owner, legislator, Stamp Act opponent, and governor. He is best remembered today, though, as the orator who spoke the words, "Give me liberty or give me death!" The manuscript of his famous 1775 Virginia Convention speech did not survive. What we know of it was reconstructed by biographer William Wirt for a book published more than forty years after the speech was given.

25 A: According to anecdotal reports, legislator Lemuel Riddick, who did not survive the year, wrote the speech, but was too ill to present it and gave it to his associate to deliver before the Convention.

26 A: It derives from Ralph Waldo Emerson's poem "Concord Hymn." Read for the first time on July 4, 1837, the opening stanza includes the lines: "Here once the embattled farmers stood / And fired the shot heard round the world."

27 Q:

Which of the following cities was never regarded as the capital of the United States?

1. Trenton
2. Baltimore
3. New York
4. Princeton
5. Boston

28 Q:

What was the first capital of the United States?

29 Q:

When was the first American submarine used in combat?

30 Q:

By now, all good trivia readers know that George Washington never chopped down that famous cherry tree. Who told the lie and why?

31 Q:

On what day did Washington cross the Delaware?

27 A:
5. The U.S. Congress met in all of the cities except for Boston.

28 A: Both New York City and Philadelphia have a claim to the honor. George Washington was inaugurated as the first president at New York's Federal Hall, and the first sessions of Congress under the Constitution were convened in that city. However, Philadelphia was considered the de facto capital at the time of the Declaration of Independence.

29 A: 1776. David Bushnell built a human-powered, one-man submarine that he called the *Turtle*. With this primitive, yet ingenious device, he hoped to sink the British warships that guarded New York Harbor with a hand-powered drill and a time bomb. He made three attempts to break the blockade, but it was all for naught. Soon thereafter, his submarine sank.

30 A: Mason Locke Weems, more commonly known as Parson Weems, told the fib about the father of our country. More specifically, he wrote this now world-famous lie in his 1800 hagiography *The Life of Washington*.

31 A: On Christmas Day in 1776, General George Washington crossed the Delaware River. The following day, he surprised and defeated the Hessians at Trenton, New Jersey. The patriots' pursuit of the German mercenaries might have been slowed by their discovery of a large cache of Hessian rum.

32 Q:

Besides Paul Revere, who else warned the good people of Concord that the British were coming?

33 Q:

Which American military leaders captured Fort Ticonderoga?

34 Q:

What was Benjamin Franklin's first pseudonym when writing for *The New England Courant*?

35 Q:

How many people were killed during the Boston Massacre?

36 Q:

Why did Crispus Attucks's name appear in the *Boston Gazette* twenty years previous to the Massacre?

32 A: Henry Wadsworth Longfellow's poem "Paul Revere's Ride" made Revere immortal, but William Dawes and Samuel Prescott also braved that midnight ride on April 18, 1775.

33 A: Americans Ethan Allen and the ill-fated Benedict Arnold surprised the British and captured Fort Ticonderoga on May 10, 1775.

34 A: Mrs. Silence Dogood. When Franklin served as a printer's apprentice for his brother James, he was refused publication in the paper, so he created the false persona of a middle-aged widow. Mrs. Dogood's letters provided a slightly satirical look at Colonial life and became quite popular. When James discovered the deceit, Ben fled to Philadelphia.

35 A: Five. Three were killed instantly (Crispus Attucks, James Caldwell, and Samuel Gray); Samuel Maverick died a few hours afterward, and Patrick Carr succumbed two weeks later.

36 A: In 1750 William Brown of Framingham had advertised for the return of a runaway slave named "Crispus"; he offered a ten pound reward. At the time of his death, Attucks had been working as a merchant seaman.

37 Q:
What started the Massacre?

38 Q:
In the weeks following the Massacre, the battle of propaganda began. One broadside printed a particularly famous and inflammatory engraving. Whose work was it?

39 Q:
Which of the thirteen original states was the first to ratify the Constitution?

40 Q:
And which was the last of the thirteen "originals" to ratify the Constitution?

41 Q:
Name the first thirteen states of the United States.

37 A: A dispute over a wigmaker's bill. Edward Garrick, a wigmaker's apprentice, demanded payment from a British officer outside the custom house. After the sentry struck the boy on the head, an argument ensued, leading to a crowd of colonists taunting the guard. As the crowd grew, British soldiers were dispatched to restore order. While the redcoats loaded their muskets, the colonists hurled snowballs and insults: The troops fired.

38 A: Paul Revere's. Entitled "The Bloody Massacre Perpetrated in King Street Boston on March 5, 1770," the widely circulated image was a colorized copy of a drawing by artist Henry Pelham. While tensions between colonists and British troops had been brewing for months, this illustration helped cement anti-British sentiment among the populace.

39 A: Delaware, which is still called the First State, ratified the document on December 7, 1787.

40 A: Rhode Island had overcome its early reluctance to join the Union by the time it agreed to the Constitution in 1790.

41 A: In the order of their statehood: Delaware, Pennsylvania, New Jersey, Georgia, Connecticut, Massachusetts, Maryland, South Carolina, New Hampshire, Virginia, New York, North Carolina, and Rhode Island.

42 Q:

We think of ourselves as American patriots, but six states were named for English kings and queens. Can you name them?

43 Q:

Everyone knows that Thomas Jefferson wrote the Declaration of Independence, but how long did it take him to write it?

44 Q:

Who sewed the first American flag?

45 Q:

Only twice in American history did two future presidents battle for the same congressional seat. Who were these contestants and who won the two races?

46 Q:

The famous *Marbury v. Madison* Supreme Court case involved one very disgruntled would-be justice of the peace. Why did this seemingly one-man affair loom so important in our nation's judicial history?

42 A: Georgia (named for George II); Maryland (for Henrietta Maria, wife of Charles I); North and South Carolina (from Carolus, Latin for the same Charles); and Virginia and West Virginia (for Elizabeth I, the Virgin Queen).

43 A: Thomas Jefferson spent eighteen days (June 11–28, 1776) drafting this historic document. In the process, he incorporated changes suggested by Benjamin Franklin and John Adams.

44 A: Betsy Ross. Some rude debunkers have claimed that the Ross flag story was made out of whole cloth, but most historians and vexillologists (flag experts) agree that the widowed seamstress did indeed create the first American flag.

45 A: James Madison and James Monroe sought the same House of Representative seat in 1789 and 1790. Madison won both times, garnering 57 percent in the first election and nearly 98 percent in the second.

46 A: In March 1801, William Marbury was one of the forty-two Federalists who had received presidential appointments on the very last day of John Adams's term in office. Thomas Jefferson, Adams's successor, refused to honor the commissions on the grounds that the paperwork had not been delivered as legally required. Marbury, who was already wealthy, pursued the case. He lost, but in its decision, John Marshall's Supreme Court forever established the judicial right to review the constitutionality of legislation.

47 Q:
How did Alexander Hamilton die?

48 Q:
What French aristocrat helped the American colonists
during the American Revolution?

49 Q:
What French pirate provided the U.S. valuable help
during the War of 1812?

50 Q:
Why did Lewis and Clark embark on their famous
expedition?

47 A: On July 11, 1804, Vice President Aaron Burr and former Secretary of the Treasury Hamilton fought a duel in Weehawken, New Jersey. Hamilton fired first, but missed, perhaps intentionally. Burr's first shot hit the Founding Father in the lower abdomen and ricocheted off a rib. Hamilton died the next day in Greenwich Village.

48 A: Marquis de Lafayette offered his military services and served as a general with the American colonists against the British during the War for Independence. He fought with distinction, particularly at the 1777 battle at Brandywine, Pennsylvania. Throughout his two extended post-war visits to the United States of America, he was treated justifiably as a hero.

49 A: Privateer and smuggler Jean Lafitte interrupted his successful pirating activities to join the fight for the United States against the British at the 1814–1815 Battle of New Orleans. For his help, Andrew Jackson personally commended Lafitte, and President James Madison issued a pardon for Lafitte and his men.

50 A: The expedition, known more officially as the Corps of Discovery, was commissioned by President Jefferson shortly after the 1803 Louisiana Purchase. The group of volunteers was led by Captain Meriwether Lewis and his good friend William Clark.

51 Q:

What was the purpose of Lewis and Clark's expedition?

52 Q:

How long did this famous trek take?

53 Q:

Did the expedition bring them fame?

54 Q:

William Clark went on to become governor of the
Missouri Territory and superintendent of Indian Affairs,
but what happened to Lewis?

51 A: Its main purpose, contrary to popular belief, was exploration and mapping, not scientific research. Thanks to the expedition, the United States laid claim to the territories of the Pacific Northwest.

52 A: Lewis, Clark, and their group left St. Louis to begin their transcontinental mission on May 14, 1804. Two and a half years later, they returned.

53 A: No, in fact, this major exploration project remained largely forgotten until the early twentieth century, when it was honored in both the 1904 St. Louis Louisiana Purchase Exposition and the 1905 Lewis and Clark Centennial Exposition in Portland.

54 A: On October 10, 1809, just three years after returning from the expedition, Meriwether Lewis retired to his bedroom at the inn after dinner. In the predawn hours, gunshots were heard, and shortly thereafter, the explorer was found with multiple wounds. He survived only a few hours. Historians continue to dispute whether it was the suicide of a despondent man or murder by land pirates.

55 Q:

Today "Tippecanoe and Tyler too" is thought of as a memorable, if confusing slogan. What was it originally and who or what are Tippecanoe and Tyler?

56 Q:

Speaking of the Battle of Tippecanoe, who was Harrison fighting and was it as great a triumph as the campaign song suggests?

55 A: Originally, they were repeated refrains in an 1840 campaign song entitled "Tip and Ty." Whig Party candidate William Henry Harrison was, by this time, well-known as the hero of the 1811 Battle of Tippecanoe. John Tyler, his vice-presidential running mate, was less well-known. It should be noted that this very popular song not only reminded voters of Harrison's wartime valor, but it also made incumbent Democrat Martin Van Buren the butt of jokes.

56 A: The battle was in December 1811 between forces led by Indiana Territory governor William Henry Harrison and warriors associated with Shawnee leader Tecumseh, who was leading a confederacy of Native Americans opposed to U.S. expansion into their territory. With an army of approximately a thousand men, Harrison attacked the Native American headquarters at Prophetstown. Tecumseh was not present; he had left on an ally-searching mission; thus his men were led by his brother, a spiritual leader who lacked battle experience. After a two-hour confrontation, the warriors, who were badly outnumbered and running low on ammunition, abandoned the fight, having inflicted more casualties than they received. Harrison and his men burned the town, but it was soon rebuilt and the struggle continued. In effect, everything remained essentially the same except that Harrison now had a campaign theme.

57 Q:
Who were the Know-Nothings and what didn't
they know?

58 Q:
How prevalent were these Nativists?

59 Q:
Which former U.S. president ran on a Nativist ticket?

60 Q:
What were Millard Fillmore's last words?

57 A: The Know-Nothings were a semi-secret organization who actively opposed Catholics, whether native-born or immigrants. This Nativist movement got its name from its code of non-disclosure: If asked about its activities, members were instructed to say, "I know nothing."

58 A: The large-scale German and Irish migrations to the U.S. between 1830 and 1850 generated widespread opposition at the polls, in state legislatures, and sometimes in the streets. Under various party names, this anti-Catholic movement magnetized the hostility of apprehensive Protestant workers, even drawing support from recent Protestant immigrants. After 1856, the movement was largely defused by the rise of the Republican Party and the intensification of debates over slavery.

59 A: Millard Fillmore, the American Party presidential candidate in 1856. The anti-Catholic ticket won one state and drew 21 percent of the vote, making it one of the best showings ever by a third-party White House ticket.

60 A: "The nourishment is palatable." According to an early news account, the thirteenth president of the United States uttered these words after tasting a soup; he expired soon thereafter.

61 Q:

What were the two aspects of William Henry Harrison's 1841 inaugural address that made it historic, if not memorable?

62 Q:

Which Founding Father wrote "History is not the Province of the Ladies," after reading Mercy Otis Warren's 1805 history of the American Revolution?

63 Q:

Later, Adams became known for the immense correspondence he shared with his wife Abigail. What did she tell him to do in her most famous letter?

64 Q:

The Autobiography of Benjamin Franklin has been called the greatest example of the genre; what was the name of Franklin's sister's memoir?

61 A: First, it was the longest inaugural address in presidential history: This tedious harangue went on for one hour and forty minutes. Second, this lackluster occasion probably killed him. Although he was sixty-eight years old and noticeably frail, Harrison insisted on delivering his lengthy address without hat, gloves, or overcoat. The combination of the brisk March weather and a downpour took its toll. Harrison became ill and never recovered. He died exactly one month after his inaugural address. Then "and Tyler too" became president.

62 A: John Adams. Warren's observations on Adams were scant and critical; he sent her a barrage of letters to complain.

63 A: "Remember the Ladies." In a letter dated March 31, 1776, Abigail encouraged her husband to include women's rights when drawing up laws for the new nation. Apparently, John did not agree.

64 A: *Book of Ages.* Jane Franklin Mecom's memoir is actually a notebook where she recorded the births and deaths of her children. Married at age fifteen, Jane had twelve children, lived in poverty, and died in obscurity. She's known because her famous brother wrote more letters to her than to anyone else; next to her notebook, she kept them all.

65 Q:

Who said the following: "We hold these truths to be self-evident, that all men and women are created equal"?

66 Q:

By how many electoral votes did John Adams defeat Thomas Jefferson in 1796?

1. 1
2. 3
3. 15
4. 23
5. 36

67 Q:

How did one president make an embarrassing discovery about the state of White House maintenance?

1. A bench in a White House sitting room collapsed under the weight of William Howard Taft.
2. Oval Office lighting problems during the Second World War forced Franklin Delano Roosevelt into the cabinet conference room.
3. Harry Truman was horrified when a piano leg poked a hole through the first-floor ceiling.
4. John F. Kennedy was given a White House tour during which his wife, Jackie, lectured him on necessary repairs.

65 A: No, it was not Thomas Jefferson. Elizabeth Cady Stanton's statement at the Women's Rights Convention in 1848 included two words missing from Jefferson's Declaration of Independence passage: "and women."

66 A:

2. Adams barely squeaked through the 1796 election, winning by only three electoral votes, 71–68. The results were decisively regional: Without solid New York and New England support, he would have been trounced by Jefferson. Even in the popular vote, he triumphed by fewer than 5,000 votes.

67 A:

3. That unplanned intrusion by the Baldwin grand piano served as a wake-up call to Truman and his executive staff.

68 Q:
Who was the first U.S. president to be born an American citizen?

69 Q:
Who is the only U.S. president who spoke English as a second language?

70 Q:
What incredibly bad pun lifted the spirits of mid-nineteenth-century Democrats?

71 Q:
Arrange these presidents in the order of their administrations:

1. William Henry Harrison
2. Martin Van Buren
3. Franklin Pierce
4. James Polk
5. Millard Fillmore

72 Q:
During one seven-year period, the United States had no vice president in office. When did this occur and why?

68 A: Martin Van Buren. All his predecessors arrived in the world as British subjects.

69 A: Martin Van Buren again. Growing up in a Dutch-speaking upstate New York community, he mastered English only later.

70 A: Supporters of Franklin Pierce couldn't resist the wince-worthy, "We will *pierce* them in 1852 as we *poked* them in 1844," the doubtful tribute being, of course, to victorious candidate James Polk.

71 A:
2., 1., 4., 5., 3.

72 A: From July 10, 1850, to March 4, 1857. After Zachary Taylor died in office, Vice President Millard Fillmore succeeded him, leaving his former job vacant. Franklin Pierce became president in 1853, but his elected vice president, William Rufus King, was nowhere to be seen. Already suffering from terminal tuberculosis, he had retreated to sunny Cuba before the inauguration. As a nonresident vice president, he survived only six weeks, dying just one day after he had returned to his Alabama plantation. Pierce served the remainder of his term without a VP.

73 Q:

For sheer gloom, one inauguration outranks all others. Who was the incoming chief executive and what were the causes of the sadness?

74 Q:

Who purportedly said, "Brady and the Cooper Institute made me president" and who and what was he talking about?

75 Q:

Did the future president really make that statement?

73 A: Franklin Pierce. Just two months before he took the oath of office, the president-elect and his wife survived a catastrophic train derailment that killed their eleven-year-old son. Pierce's wife viewed the tragedy as divine punishment for her husband's pursuit of the high office. To make matters worse, the vice president was gravely ill and could not attend the swearing-in ceremony. (See previous question.) To place a headstone on the grim event, Abigail Fillmore, the wife of the outgoing president, caught a bad cold at the outdoor ceremony and died only a month later.

74 A: Unemployed Republican legislator Abraham Lincoln was not yet a presidential candidate when he gave a powerful speech about slavery at New York City's Cooper Institute (now called Cooper Union) in late February 1860. Earlier in the day, he had his photograph taken at Mathew Brady's nearby Broadway studio. The nearly simultaneous widespread distribution of the speech and reproductions of the full-length photograph helped give Lincoln a national reputation and pave his way to the White House.

75 A: Probably not. Mathew Brady was a talented self-promoter who successfully sought out celebrities (more than a dozen presidents were photographed in his studios), but he also was not above the occasional fib. For instance, he offered detailed memories of a studio session of Edgar Allan Poe in which the moody poet read him an early draft of "The Raven." The incident almost certainly never occurred.

76 Q:

How many presidents have been named George?

1. 1
2. 2
3. 3
4. 4
5. 5

77 Q:

The brother of a presidential assassin once saved the son of the man his brother killed. Can you identify the principals in this strange reversal of history?

78 Q:

Who was Abraham Lincoln's powerful opponent in the electoral contest that brought him to the White House in 1860?

1. Stephen A. Douglas
2. John C. Breckinridge
3. John Bell
4. John C. Crittenden

76 A:
3. Just three. Two were Bushes (George H. W. and George W.) and the other was the father of our country (George Washington).

77 A: In 1863 or 1864, Abraham Lincoln's eldest son, Robert, was returning from a college break at Harvard when he and John Wilkes Booth's brother Edwin happened to be on the same crowded train platform in Jersey City, New Jersey. (Ironically, Edwin, one of the most famous actors of his time, was traveling that day with the owner of Ford's Theatre.) In the crush of the throng, young Robert was knocked off the platform, but as he fell, Booth grabbed his coat collar, saving him from major injury or perhaps death on the tracks.

78 A:
2. Breckinridge, Bell, and Douglas all carried states in this very regional election, but it was Breckinridge's electoral control of the South that made him Lincoln's most formidable rival. Perhaps surprisingly, Douglas, the best known to modern readers, finished fourth in the electoral votes, although he did finish second in the popular vote.

79 Q:

In his private journal, a president wrote about "a dull young man, with a loud voice, trying to pound some noise in the question." Who was the president and about whom was he writing?

80 Q:

"Each public officer who takes an oath to support the Constitution swears that he will support it as he understands it, and not as it is understood by others." Which very opinionated chief executive wrote these words?

1. Andrew Jackson
2. Theodore Roosevelt
3. Harry S. Truman
4. Grover Cleveland
5. James A. Garfield

81 Q:

Identify the presidents behind these quotations:

1. "The White House is a bully pulpit."
2. "What we believe in is what works."
3. "There are a number of things wrong with Washington. One of them is that everyone has been too long away from home."
4. "I want a kinder, gentler nation."
5. "I like the noise of democracy."

79 A: James A. Garfield, in reference to Charles Guiteau, who within weeks would become the president's assassin. Garfield was alluding to the disappointed office seeker's disruption of a sermon that the president and his wife had just attended. (Guiteau had hoped to kill the president in a church to ensure his victim's heavenly passage.)

80 A:
1. Judging by his political skirmishes, Old Hickory lived out his beliefs.

81 A:
1. Theodore Roosevelt.
2. Bill Clinton.
3. Dwight D. Eisenhower.
4. George H. W. Bush.
5. James Buchanan.

82 Q:

Which president waged the Mexican-American War?

1. James Buchanan
2. James A. Garfield
3. James Polk
4. John Tyler
5. Zachary Taylor

83 Q:

Alexander Graham Bell is justly renowned as the father of the telephone (and thus telecommunications), but he also very nearly saved the life of a U.S. president. Who was the president and why did Bell's attempt fail?

84 Q:

The most famous political speech in American history was delivered at a Democratic National Convention, but its rousing words were delivered by a perpetual candidate who never won the White House. What was the speech called and who was the luckless orator?

82 A:

3. James Polk's one-term presidency (1845–1849) was marked by territorial disputes, domestic discord, and a bloody war that killed 70,000 Americans and Mexicans—but he did find time to be the earliest sitting president to be photographed in the White House.

83 A: Charles Guiteau's 1881 assassination attempt left President James A. Garfield with a bullet embedded in his chest. With X-rays still not invented, it could only be located with manual instrument probes that raised the risk of infection. Reading news accounts of the presidential predicament, Bell realized that a metal-detecting device that he had developed might help. His apparatus worked in tests on Civil War veterans, but ended up failing in his two attempts to save Garfield at the White House. The reason was simple: Unbeknownst to the inventor, Garfield's bed had metal coil springs, which were extremely uncommon at the time. Had Bell known, he might been able to save the president, who died just a few weeks later.

84 A: William Jennings Bryan was a thirty-six-year-old Nebraska congressman when he brought the 1896 convention to its feet with his "Cross of Gold" speech. His call of "You shall not crucify mankind on a cross of gold" won favor from debt-ridden farmers and other cash-poor voters. Bryan's ardent call for monetary reform helped make him the party's presidential candidate in 1896, 1900, and 1908, but it never got him elected.

85 Q:
Which president fancied having his head rubbed with petroleum jelly as he ate breakfast?

86 Q:
It is common knowledge that Ronald Reagan's favorite food was jelly beans. What flavor did the Jelly Belly Company create especially for the president's inauguration?

87 Q:
How many pounds of jelly beans were ordered by the White House during the Reagan administration?

88 Q:
How many presidents got married during their executive term of office, and how many of them were married in a White House ceremony?

1. 1 and 1
2. 2 and 0
3. 3 and 1
4. 4 and 1
5. 4 and 2

85 A: This somewhat kinky-sounding pleasure was favored by Calvin Coolidge.

86 A: Blueberry; so that Reagan could have red, white, and blue jelly beans.

87 A: To satisfy Ronald Reagan's well-known passion for the chewy stuff, 24,000 pounds of jelly beans were ordered—and presumably consumed—by the staff of the White House during his two terms.

88 A:
3. The three presidential grooms were John Tyler, Grover Cleveland, and Woodrow Wilson, but only Cleveland was married in a White House ceremony.

89 Q:

How many presidents were widowed while in office?

1. 2
2. 3
3. 4
4. 5
5. 6

90 Q:

How many presidents entered the White House without a spouse?

1. 1
2. 2
3. 3
4. 4
5. 5

91 Q:

Which future presidents graduated from West Point?

92 Q:

How many future presidents graduated from Annapolis?

89 A:

1 and 2. There are two possible answers. John Tyler and Woodrow Wilson both lost their first wives while they were in office. As we know from the previous entry, both married again before leaving the presidency. Andrew Jackson, the third widower, is a more difficult case: He lost his beloved spouse when he was still president-elect, before he had taken the oath of office.

90 A:

5. Four early presidents had been married and widowed before they reached the highest office: Thomas Jefferson, Andrew Jackson, Martin Van Buren, and Chester A. Arthur. (Significantly, all four workaholic husbands deeply mourned their wives and none of them ever remarried.) James Buchanan, the fifth spouseless arrival at the White House, was the only lifelong bachelor who has served as president.

91 A: Ulysses S. Grant, class of 1843, and Dwight D. Eisenhower, class of 1915, both earned diplomas from the United States Military Academy.

92 A: Only one. Jimmy Carter graduated from the United States Naval Academy in 1946.

93 Q:

How many U.S. presidents went to Yale?

1. 1
2. 2
3. 3
4. 4
5. 5
6. 6

94 Q:

How many U.S. presidents went to Harvard?

1. 4
2. 5
3. 6
4. 7
5. 8
6. 9

95 Q:

How many U.S. presidents earned a Ph.D.?

1. 1
2. 2
3. 3
4. 4
5. 5

93 A:

5. In chronological order, they are Presidents William Howard Taft, Gerald Ford, George H. W. Bush, Bill Clinton, and George W. Bush.

94 A:

5. They are Presidents John Adams, John Quincy Adams, Rutherford B. Hayes, Theodore Roosevelt, Franklin Delano Roosevelt, John F. Kennedy, George W. Bush, and Barack Obama. Patriot and master penman John Hancock also attended Harvard.

95 A:

1. Only Woodrow Wilson, who received his doctorate at Johns Hopkins University in 1886. Several recent presidents, including Jimmy Carter, Bill Clinton, George W. Bush, and Barack Obama, have had impressive post-graduate credentials, but none can match the academic credentials of this predecessor. Wilson was not only a professor at Princeton University, he also became its president, and his academic works were widely respected and read. Not bad for someone who didn't learn to read until he was eleven.

96 Q:

One American president was a former prisoner of war.
Name him and the war.

97 Q:

What president remained illiterate until adulthood and
was once the subject of a wanted poster?

98 Q:

Which president had the most children?

1. John Tyler
2. John Adams
3. Thomas Jefferson
4. William Harrison
5. Rutherford B. Hayes

99 Q:

Who was Leslie Lynch King, Jr.?

100 Q:

How many presidents' last names have only four letters?

1. 2
2. 3
3. 4
4. 5
5. 6

96 A: Future commander-in-chief Andrew Jackson was a teenager when he and his brother were captured by British troops during the Revolutionary War.

97 A: Andrew Johnson grew up in poverty in Raleigh, North Carolina, and was only ten when his family apprenticed him to a local tailor. When he and his brother ran away from their master five years later, the tailor offered a ten dollar reward for their capture. With his wife's encouragement and help, the future president learned to read, write, and improve his mathematical skills.

98 A:
1. John Tyler had fifteen children, eight with his first wife, Letitia Christian Tyler, and seven with his second wife, Julia Gardiner Tyler. There are assertions that the tenth president also fathered at least one son by a slave, but to date, those claims have not been confirmed.

99 A: The birth name of president Gerald R. Ford Jr. His mother took Gerald Rudolff Ford as her second husband shortly before her son's second birthday, and the future president was given his stepfather's name, although he spelled his middle name as "Rudolph."

100 A:
5. The quintet consists of James Polk, William Howard Taft, Gerald Ford, George H. W. Bush, and George W. Bush.

101 Q:
What was Bill Clinton's birth name?

102 Q:
For whom was the teddy bear named?

103 Q:
Which president gave the shortest inauguration address?

104 Q:
Eight presidents were born in one state. Can you identify the state and the presidents?

101 A: William Jefferson Blythe III. Clinton's natural father died in an automobile accident before his son's birth. Four years later, Virginia Cassidy Blythe married Roger Clinton. When the future president was fifteen, he adopted the name of his stepfather.

102 A: President Theodore "Teddy" Roosevelt, of course. While on a hunting trip in 1902, Teddy insisted that the hunting party put a wounded bear out of its misery. Eventually, with the help of cartoonist Clifford Berryman, the story changed to Teddy "rescuing" a wounded bear cub. Shortly thereafter, enterprising toy manufacturers gave these stuffed animals the endearing name.

103 A: George Washington's second inaugural speech lasted only two minutes. It consisted of a mere 133 words.

104 A: Virginia. The eight presidents born within its borders were Washington, Jefferson, Madison, Monroe, William Henry Harrison, Tyler, Taylor, and Wilson. The runner-up state is Ohio, with seven presidential births: Grant, Hayes, Garfield, Benjamin Harrison, McKinley, Taft, and Harding.

105 Q:

Which beleaguered American president quipped, "If one morning I walked on top of the water across the Potomac, the headline that afternoon would read 'PRESIDENT CAN'T SWIM!'"?

1. Richard Nixon
2. Lyndon B. Johnson
3. Ronald Reagan
4. Harry S. Truman
5. Franklin Delano Roosevelt

106 Q:

Which vice president vented his job frustration thusly: "My country has in its wisdom contrived for me the most insignificant office that ever the invention of man contrived or his imagination conceived"?

1. Theodore Roosevelt
2. John Adams
3. John Nance Garner
4. Joe Biden
5. Thomas R. Marshall

107 Q:

As vice president, how many times did Harry S. Truman meet with President Franklin Delano Roosevelt?

105 A:

2. Perhaps LBJ was just having a bad day.

106 A:

2. America's first vice president obviously didn't care much for his job. Fortunately for him, he soon got a promotion: He became our second president.

107 A: According to Roosevelt's appointment calendar, only twice. It should be noted, however, that Truman served as vice president for less than two months before becoming the leader of the land.

108 Q:

What ringing comment did Harry S. Truman make concerning friendship in Washington, D.C.?

109 Q:

Two U.S. presidents suffered the embarrassing experience of having their vice president shoot someone while in office. Who were they?

110 Q:

Match the president with the name of his domestic program.

1. Franklin Delano Roosevelt   a. Fair Deal
2. Theodore Roosevelt   b. New Frontier
3. John F. Kennedy   c. New Freedom
4. Harry S. Truman   d. New Deal
5. Woodrow Wilson   e. Square Deal

111 Q:

Who was the youngest man to become president?

112 Q:

Who was the oldest man to be president?

108 A: According to White House correspondent Helen Thomas, Truman said, "If you want a friend in Washington, get a dog."

109 A: Thomas Jefferson and George W. Bush. Jefferson's vice president Aaron Burr shot and killed Alexander Hamilton in an 1804 duel. Dick Cheney, Bush's VP, hadn't intended to injure his victim; with an errant shot, he accidentally wounded seventy-eight-year-old Texas attorney Harry Whittington while the two were quail-hunting together in early 2006.

110 A:
1 and d.
2 and e.
3 and b.
4 and a.
5 and c.

111 A: Theodore Roosevelt was forty-two when he stepped into the presidency in 1901 after William McKinley's assassination. John F. Kennedy was the youngest person *elected* president, taking the oath of office when he was just forty-three.

112 A: When he left office in 1989, Ronald Reagan was seventy-seven years old.

113 Q:

What was Ronald Reagan's last acting stint before he turned his attention to politics?

114 Q:

What was the largest gathering of U.S. presidents, past, present, and future?

1. 3 presidents
2. 4 presidents
3. 5 presidents
4. 6 presidents
5. 7 presidents

115 Q:

When did such a gathering first occur?

1. at the Eisenhower funeral
2. at the Nixon funeral
3. at the dedication of Ronald Reagan's library
4. at Ronald Reagan's funeral
5. at the White House, when outgoing President George W. Bush welcomed president-elect Barack Obama to the "President's Club"

116 Q:

Name the state capitals named after American presidents.

113 A: During the 1964–1965 season, Reagan hosted *Death Valley Days*, sometimes doubling as an actor in the episode.

114 A:
3. Five presidents.

115 A:
2. Five chief executives attended the 1994 funeral of Richard Nixon: President Clinton and former presidents Ford, Carter, Reagan, and George H. W. Bush. Subsequently, five presidents were present at the occasions noted in answers 3, 4, and 5.

116 A: There are four: Jackson, Mississippi; Jefferson City, Missouri; Lincoln, Nebraska; and Madison, Wisconsin. Of course, hundreds of other American towns and cities have been named after presidents.

117 Q:
Why isn't Cleveland, Ohio, on the list of state capitals named after presidents?

118 Q:
Only three presidential candidates won at least 520 electoral votes in their race for the White House. Who are they?

119 Q:
Name the four chief executives who won the White House after being defeated as presidential candidates.

120 Q:
John Adams, John Quincy Adams, Grover Cleveland, William McKinley, Gerald Ford, William Howard Taft, George H. W. Bush, Benjamin Harrison, Martin Van Buren, Herbert Hoover, and Jimmy Carter: Of these eleven presidents, all but one was defeated when seeking re-election—but that lone exception was also the most unlucky. Who is he and why?

121 Q:
Who was the shortest American president?

117 A: For two reasons: It isn't Ohio's capital city (Columbus is), and it wasn't named after President Grover Cleveland. The city's name honors General Moses Cleaveland, the eighteenth-century surveyor who is credited with laying out the settlement's downtown plan. Immediately after he finished the job, he returned to his Connecticut home and never visited the region again.

118 A: Franklin Delano Roosevelt garnered 523 in 1936; Richard Nixon, 520 in 1972; and Ronald Reagan, 525 in 1984. Each of them was running for a second term.

119 A: Thomas Jefferson, Andrew Jackson, William Henry Harrison, and Richard Nixon. Sixteen years before Franklin Delano Roosevelt became president in 1936, he had been defeated as a vice-presidential candidate.

120 A: Unlike the others, William McKinley was reelected, but unlike the others, he didn't survive. He was assassinated less than a year after he won a second term.

121 A: James Madison stood only five feet four inches tall. He was probably also the lightest American president in history, weighing in at only a hundred pounds.

122 Q:
Who was the tallest American president and who was
the heaviest?

123 Q:
Speaking of bathtubs, H. L. Mencken once single-
handedly engineered an indoor plumbing hoax.
Can you flush it out?

124 Q:
Which U.S. president kept a raccoon named Rebecca as
a White House pet?

125 Q:
During which administration were electric lights added
to the White House?

122 A: Abraham Lincoln was six feet four inches, but weight-wise, he was no match for the 335-pound William Howard Taft. According to an often-told, but probably apocryphal story, Taft once became hopelessly stuck while taking a bath in the White House. It is said that it took six men to extricate the naked commander-in-chief.

123 A: In 1917, the famed Baltimore journalist wrote a much-quoted column that asserted that President Millard Fillmore installed the first bathtub in the White House. By the time Mencken confessed the ruse ten years later, his story had gained wide acceptance. To this day, it remains unclear who was the first U.S. president to become totally clean.

124 A: Calvin Coolidge. The furry little critter had been sent to the president by Mississippian backers as a dinner entree, but "Silent Cal" decided to adopt it as a pet. Rebecca wasn't the only four-legged creature in the Coolidge White House: The commander-in-chief also made pets of a bear, a donkey, a bobcat, a lion, and a hippo.

125 A: Benjamin Harrison's. The executive illumination began in 1891, but the president's fear of electrocution kept him from personally operating the new lights.

126 Q:
Who made the first presidential phone call?

127 Q:
Who installed a bowling alley in the White House?

128 Q:
On June 2, 1886, a historic event occurred at the White House. What was it?

129 Q:
What does the "S" in Harry S. Truman's name stand for?

130 Q:
How many U.S. presidents were born in the great state of Texas?

1. 1
2. 2
3. 3
4. 4
5. 5

126 A: Rutherford B. Hayes had a telephone installed in the White House in 1879. Perhaps appropriately, its phone number was "1." It would be a full half-century, however, before Herbert Hoover would install the first telephone in the Oval Office.

127 A: Thirty-seventh president Richard Nixon and his equally avid bowler wife had an alley installed in an underground space in 1969. In 1947, President Harry Truman had received a bowling alley as a White House birthday gift, but he essentially ignored the gift and eventually it was moved.

128 A: That day, for the first and only time, a U.S. president was married in the White House: Grover Cleveland wed Frances Folsom in the Blue Room. Cleveland was twenty-seven years older than his new bride; he had known the only child of his former law partner since she was a toddler.

129 A: Absolutely nothing. To his grandfathers Anderson Shipp Truman and Solomon Young, the lone initial probably seemed like an even-handed tribute.

130 A:
2. Only two: Lyndon B. Johnson and Dwight D. Eisenhower. George H. W. Bush and George W. Bush seem logical choices because they were Texas residents when elected, but both were New England–born.

131 Q:
Who was the first president to take up golf?

132 Q:
Identify these presidential baseball firsts:

1. the first president to invite an amateur baseball team to the White House
2. the first to invite a professional team to the White House
3. the first to invite a major league team to the White House
4. the first to throw out the first pitch on Opening Day
5. the first to call a broadcasted play-by-play while in office

133 Q:
Who was the first oath-taker to ride to his presidential inaugural in an automobile?

131 A: William Howard Taft. To become the first White House occupant who played the game, the corpulent Ohio Republican ignored religious protests, mockery of his girth, and comments from his mentor/predecessor Teddy Roosevelt. It's possible that TR himself had played golf, but he had been careful to distance himself publicly from the activity that he dismissed as a "game of snobs and dudes." Whatever the case, at some personal cost Taft inspired an American golf boom with his enthusiastic play.

132 A:
1. Andrew Johnson in 1865.
2. Ulysses S. Grant, who hosted the Cincinnati Red Stockings in 1869.
3. Chester Arthur, who invited the National League's Cleveland Forest City in 1883.
4. William Howard Taft to future Hall-of-Famer Walter Johnson in 1910.
5. Ronald Reagan in 1988. (He was also the first commander-in-chief to watch a major league game from the dugout.)

133 A: Warren Harding was driven to his 1921 inaugural in a quite horseless buggy.

134 Q:
One U.S. president was arrested for vehicular homicide.
Who was he?

135 Q:
Which former U.S. president joined the Confederacy?

136 Q:
Name the presidents portrayed on Mount Rushmore.

137 Q:
Bill Clinton, Barack Obama, George H. W. Bush,
Harry S. Truman, Ronald Reagan, James A. Garfield,
and Gerald Ford share one of these things. What is it?

1. They all won their first term by small margins.
2. They were all presidents within the past hundred years.
3. They all preferred fiction to nonfiction.
4. They were all left-handed.

134 A: On a blustery afternoon in 1833, Franklin Pierce was returning to the Executive Mansion after visiting a friend. Just seconds after he ordered his driver to speed up, his horse-drawn carriage ran over and killed an elderly woman. A Washington constable rushed to the scene and arrested Pierce for vehicular murder. Pierce claimed that as president, he was beyond the reach of the law, but the charge stuck until witnesses assured police officials that the accident had been unavoidable.

135 A: Virginian John Tyler had been the tenth president of the United States, but he was later elected as a delegate to the Congress of the Confederacy in 1861. He died, however, before he could take his seat. This rebellious deed earned an unprecedented silence: His death, unlike those of all his presidential predecessors, was not announced by the White House.

136 A: From viewer's left to right: George Washington, Thomas Jefferson, Theodore Roosevelt, Abraham Lincoln.

137 A:
4. There have also been claims that Herbert Hoover was left-handed, but to date, they have not been substantiated.

138 Q:

Five of our seven most recent presidents have been southpaws. That compares with what percentage of left-handers in the general population?

1. 5 percent
2. 10 percent
3. 15 percent
4. 20 percent
5. 25 percent

139 Q:

In which recent elections were both or all major presidential candidates left-handed?

1. 1992
2. 1996
3. 2000
4. 2004
5. 2008

138 A:

2. According to scientific research, only approximately 10 percent of people are left-handed. Thus, the 71 percent proportion of lefties among recent U.S. presidents far exceeds that of the American populous.

139 A:

1, 2, and 5. In 1992, lefties George H. W. Bush, Bill Clinton, and Ross Perot competed for the White House. Four years later, Clinton and Perot were joined by Bob Dole, who learned to use his left hand after his right hand was paralyzed by a World War II injury. In the 2008 contest, Barack Obama and John McCain extended the trend of all-southpaw White House aspirants.

140 Q:

Several presidents are said to have been natural left-handers who were forced or encouraged to become righties when they were growing up. Which of these heads of state fits that description?

1. George W. Bush
2. Ronald Reagan
3. James A. Garfield
4. Gerald Ford
5. Harry S. Truman

141 Q:

Did the Monroe Doctrine promise to expel all European colonizers from the Americas?

140 A:
2, 3, 4, and 5. It is possible that some other presidents made a similar switch early in life.

141 A: No. Contrary to popular belief, President James Monroe's decree of December 2, 1823, stated only that any further efforts by nations to colonize land or interfere with states in the Americas would be viewed as acts of aggression that required U.S. intervention. The doctrine explicitly acknowledged, however, that the United States would not interfere with existing European colonies.

142 Q:
Ford, Reagan, and Garfield all earned ambidextrous credentials, but of the three, one of them was capable of feats that topped them all. Who was he and what could he do?

1. When signing piles of executive orders, Ford would frequently switch between hands to avoid tiredness.
2. Reagan astounded friends by his near-identical handwriting with either hand.
3. Garfield was known as a very rapid penman with either hand.
4. It was famously said that Gerald Ford was left-handed sitting down and right-handed standing up.
5. Garfield could write Greek with one hand and Latin with the other—simultaneously!

143 Q:
When did the Monroe Doctrine first gain its name?

144 Q:
At the time when President Monroe made his famous State of the Union pronouncement, the United States probably didn't possess the military might to enforce its ambitious provisions. Why then did the decree become so famous?

142 A:
5. Most modern Americans, of course, would be surprised that any U.S. president could write in Greek or Latin at all.

143 A: Oddly, it wasn't until 1853 that the Monroe Doctrine became known as the Monroe Doctrine.

144 A: Simply put, this somewhat wordy proclamation has served as a convenient precedent for American foreign policy aspirations and objections near and far. In fact, the Monroe Doctrine has been invoked for matters involving Texas, Oregon, Cuba, Venezuela, and even Hawaii.

145 Q:

What is the so-called Roosevelt Corollary?

146 Q:

Was the Corollary nothing more than a rhetorical assertion?

147 Q:

If Teddy Roosevelt's Corollary turned the Monroe Doctrine on its head, what did Franklin Delano Roosevelt's reset do?

148 Q:

Who did Andrew Jackson mockingly call "Miss Nancy" and "Aunt Fancy"?

149 Q:

On July 4, 1826, the United States celebrated its fiftieth birthday. What else made that day memorable?

145 A: In his own State of the Union speech of 1904, President Theodore Roosevelt put an imaginative twist on the Monroe Doctrine. He asserted that not only did the U.S. have the right to keep Europeans out of the Americas; we also had the right to intervene in other countries in the Western Hemisphere to keep them out.

146 A: On the contrary, over the next few decades, it was used as a rationale for numerous extended "international police" interventions, including Cuba (1906–1909); Nicaragua (1909–1910 and 1912–1925); Haiti (1915–1934); the Dominican Republic (1916–1924); and Nicaragua (1926–1933).

147 A: FDR's Good Neighbor Policy of 1933 declared, in the words of his Secretary of State, that: "No country has the right to intervene in the internal or external affairs of another." Thus, Roosevelt's explicit opposition to armed intervention effectively retracted the fangs of the Monroe Doctrine's most hawkish advocates.

148 A: The former president's homophobic taunt was made toward future U.S. president James Buchanan and his live-in friend William Rufus King. Many contemporaries and several historians concluded that these "Siamese twin" constant companions were indeed gay.

149 A: Former presidents John Adams and Thomas Jefferson both died that day. Five years later—also on Independence Day—James Monroe died.

150 Q:

The last words spoken by one of those presidents that day hold a rare poignancy. What did John Adams say?

151 Q:

How did naval commander Stephen Decatur die?

1. He died as the last man leaving the burning USS *Philadelphia* during the Barbary War.
2. He was killed attempting to escape the British blockade at New London.
3. He died quietly in Washington's Lafayette Square after retiring from an active shipboard life.
4. He was wounded and died shortly after a duel in Maryland.
5. He succumbed to a disease (perhaps typhus) during the Tripolitan campaign.

152 Q:

How long did the defenders of the Alamo successfully hold out?

150 A: "Thomas Jefferson survives." Given the communication of the time, the ninety-year-old Founding Father could not have known that eighty-three-year-old Jefferson had died in Monticello just a few hours earlier.

151 A:
4. Ironically, after surviving numerous bloody naval battles, Decatur died at the hands of a fellow American military leader. Early in his career, he was a judge at the court-martial that convicted Commodore James Barron. After Decatur repeatedly resisted the commodore's attempts at reinstatement, Barron challenged him to a duel. On March 22, 1820, the two met on the field and exchanged gunfire at a close distance. Both were wounded, Decatur mortally.

152 A: Almost two weeks. A more flippant answer might be, "Thirteen days and more than a dozen films." In real-life 1836, these approximately 190 brave defenders were hopelessly outnumbered by 1,500 Mexican troops.

153 Q:

For which of the following is Stephen Decatur rightly remembered?

1. He was the first post–Revolutionary War naval hero.
2. He uttered the famous words, "My country, right or wrong."
3. His wife chose him over suitors that included Aaron Burr and Napoleon's younger brother.
4. His gallant shipboard service during the War of 1812 and two Barbary Wars.
5. His active participation in the design and building of ships for the early U.S. Navy.

154 Q:

Was the Alamo a formidable fortress?

155 Q:

"Don't give up the ship!" was the dying plea of a naval commander. Name him:

1. John Paul Jones
2. James Lawrence
3. Stephen Decatur
4. Jacob Jones
5. David Porter

153 A:
1, 3, 4, and 5. Decatur is often credited with asserting, "My country, right or wrong," but what he actually said while delivering a toast at a Washington social gathering was somewhat different: "Our Country! In her intercourse with foreign nations may she always be in the right; but right or wrong, our country!" It was German-born statesman Carl Schurz who distilled the affirmation, thus making it famous.

154 A: No, this abandoned and then restructured eighteenth-century Catholic mission was, as victorious General Antonio López de Santa Anna described it, an "irregular fortification hardly worthy of the name."

155 A:
2. James Lawrence had been only recently promoted to captain when he took command of the USS *Chesapeake* during the War of 1812. In a fierce battle with British block-aders off the coast of Massachusetts, he was severely wounded by small arms fire. Taken below, he spoke these quotable words. He died three days late on June 4, 1813.

156 Q:

How did his sailors respond to his calls of "Don't give up the ship!" and "Fight her till she sinks!"

1. They repulsed the attack of the HMS *Shannon* and returned safely to port.
2. Though their masts were burning and some of their cannons were disabled, they sank the Royal Naval frigate.
3. After a protracted battle, the *Shannon* surrendered and was towed back to Boston Harbor.
4. Both ships were badly damaged, but Americans regarded it as a moral victory because the blockade had, in effect, been broken.
5. The *Chesapeake* surrendered and its sailors were imprisoned.

157 Q:

When did the Erie Canal open?

158 Q:

Why was the canal so important?

159 Q:

Who paid for it?

156 A:
5. The defeat sounds humiliating, but the *Chesapeake* had been roundly trounced by the thirty-eight-gun British frigate. Nor did the officers and sailors yield quietly: Sixty of them died in the encounter and sixty others were injured, some of them gravely.

157 A: The first canal boat left Buffalo on October 26, 1825, and arrived in New York City on November 4. By connecting Lake Erie to the Hudson River, the canal radically decreased the shipping time between cities in the interior and the Atlantic coast.

158 A: To contemporary travelers, a 363-mile waterway that took an average of ten days to traverse doesn't seem like an epoch-making creation, but in the nineteenth century, the Erie Canal changed the face of America. The first water transportation system between the Eastern seaboard and the Great Lakes cut transportation costs by about 95 percent and gave New York City and New York State unprecedented national importance.

159 A: New York State picked up the $7 million construction tab. Its success forever silenced the critics of the eight-year project who had lambasted it as "[Governor Dewitt] Clinton's ditch."

160 Q:

In 1807, a New York portrait painter stunned the world with the first commercial use of a great invention. What was his name and what was his brainchild?

1. Benjamin Thompson Rumford and the coffee percolator
2. Edward Hicks and the muzzle-loading cannon
3. Robert Fulton and the steam-powered boat
4. Samuel F. B. Morse and the telegraph
5. Oliver Evans and the vapor-compression refrigeration process

161 Q:

How rapidly could this new invention traverse the 150-mile Erie Canal voyage between New York City and Albany?

1. 12 hours
2. 15 hours
3. 26 hours
4. 32 hours
5. 38 hours

160 A:

3. Other inventors could claim primacy for devising steam-powered vessels, but it was Fulton who made such travel economically viable. In 1807, he and his friend Robert R. Livingston together built the first commercial steamboat. Fulton is best remembered today as an innovator, but he was also a well-trained artist, having apprenticed under prominent historical painter Benjamin West.

161 A:

4. This grueling day-and-a-half trip might exhaust today's travelers, but their nineteenth-century equivalents were apparently enthralled.

162 Q:

Which of these inventions did the ever-industrous Fulton design and/or perfect?

1. the first working submarine
2. the first modern naval torpedoes
3. the first panorama shown in Paris
4. a system of inland waterways
5. a steam warship

163 Q:

Who was Charles Sherwood Stratton—and how did he become so famous?

164 Q:

In February 1863, war-exhausted Americans reveled in a unique New York City wedding. Who were the bride and groom and how many attended the gala?

165 Q:

Was the marriage successful? Did they have children?

162 A:
1, 2, 3, 4, and 5.

163 A: Charles Stratton, known worldwide as Tom Thumb, was a very talented little person. Stratton was three foot four, but would not have achieved his international acclaim without his quick wit, his ample performing skills, and the marketing genius of P. T. Barnum.

164 A: Lower Manhattan's high-society Grace Episcopal Church was the site of the nuptials between Charles Stratton (aka Tom Thumb) and Lavinia Warren (formerly Lavinia Warren Bumpus), a woman of short stature. Barnum little-people performer "Commodore Nutt" and Lavinia's younger sister Minnie served as best man and maid of honor. More than 2,000 people attended the wedding. President Abraham Lincoln was, of course, occupied with other matters, but he did send a gift and invite them to the White House. At the reception, Tom and Lavinia remained on a platform to avoid being trampled by the appreciative crowd.

165 A: The happy couple remained married for twenty years until Stratton's death in 1883. They had no children, but did sometimes pose with infants for commercial photographs. Two years after her beloved husband's death, Lavinia married Count Primo Magri, an Italian dwarf aristocrat.

166 Q:

Who famously said, "There's a sucker born every minute"?

167 Q:

Did Barnum ever serve in an elected office?

168 Q:

Where was oil first discovered in the United States?

169 Q:

The melodrama *Mazeppa* and its female star Adah Isaacs Menken caused a sensation when it opened in New York in 1860. Why?

1. A very live, galloping horse was featured in the drama.
2. The male lead was played by the short-haired, androgynous-looking Menken.
3. In one scene, the attractive actress appeared briefly in flesh-colored tights.
4. The play was based on a poem by Byron.
5. With her multiple husbands, affairs, and flagrant cigarette-smoking, Menken was a magnet for scandal.

166 A: This derogatory claim remains inextricably attached to showman P. T. Barnum, but there is no proof that this buoyant huckster actually made the remark. In fact, it seems much more probable that it was made by a competitor or a critic. In his circus and traveling exhibits, Barnum did present real acts, including the original Siamese twins Chang and Eng and performing little people such as Tom Thumb, but he also sponsored outright hoaxes. Among the most famous were his fake ten-foot Cardiff Giant, a "Feejee mermaid," and Joice Heth, an elderly African-American woman who he hawked as the 161-year-old former nurse of George Washington.

167 A: Yes. Against some expectations, he was elected to the Connecticut state legislature in 1865. Phineas Taylor Barnum had also served as the mayor of Bridgeport, Connecticut.

168 A: The first oil well was drilled in Titusville, Pennsylvania, by Colonel Edwin L. Drake in August 1859. Its presence in the area was known before that time; in fact, it was already used medicinally for both animals and humans. The discovery set off a Pennsylvania oil rush that peaked in the early 1890s.

169 A: All of the above are true; of those, the Byron connection was probably the least cause of its notoriety. In any case, Menken took the play to London and Paris, where its popularity was repeated.

170 Q:

Who was John C. Heenan?

1. He was an Irish-born ruffian.
2. He was a bare-knuckle boxer who was accepted as the American champion even though he had only three formal fights during his entire career, and he lost two of them. The third ended in a draw.
3. In England, he fought what is generally regarded as the first world championship. On his return to the States, he was treated as a hero.
4. He had a short, bigamous marriage to notorious actress Adah Isaacs Menken.

171 Q:

The Oregon Trail has been called the most important footpath on the continent. What is it and what makes it so significant?

170 A:

2, 3, and **4.** Heenan might have been a ruffian, but this son of County Tipperary parents was born and bred in West Troy (now Watervliet), New York. As a teenager, he went to California during the Gold Rush days, but came back to New York when a boxing manager recognized his fighting ability. As the pugilist now known as the "Benicia Boy," he became the American champion when his long-time foe, thug and street brawler John Morrissey retired. Almost immediately, he challenged the British champion, Tommy Sayers. When they fought in England in 1860, the illegal bout ended in a riot and a bloody draw. After just one more fight, Heenan returned to America, where he died at the tender age of thirty-nine.

171 A: This 2,000-mile trail runs from Independence, Missouri, to the Columbia River region in Oregon. The trail generally follows the Platte River to its headwaters, crosses the mountains, and then snakes along the Snake River to the Columbia River. It was a path first used by Native Americans, fur traders, and missionaries, but beginning in 1842, wagon trains rolled westward in massive numbers. Over the next twenty-five years, more than half a million people traveled this overland route, which became less important when the transcontinental railroad was completed in 1869.

172 Q:

All astute trivia buffs know that Eli Whitney invented the cotton gin. But what is a cotton gin and why was the invention so important?

173 Q:

When did the so-called "Era of Good Feelings" begin?

1. 1806
2. 1816
3. 1826
4. 1836
5. 1846

174 Q:

How did the term originate?

1. Monroe himself used the phrase in a speech given on a two-year country-wide goodwill tour that began in 1817.
2. The descriptive phrase was bestowed by a sympathetic Federalist newspaper editor.
3. The term seemed a natural reflection of post–War of 1812 sentiments in the states.
4. Later historians coined the phrase, using it derisively because of the often-concealed factionalism both between parties and inside the Monroe administration itself.

172 A: Whitney's 1794 "engine" (or "gin") enabled plantation owners to separate the sticky green seeds from the short staple cotton fiber in an efficient and cost-effective way. Thanks to Whitney's invention, the yield of raw cotton in the South doubled for several decades after 1800.

173 A:
3. With the presidential election of James Monroe.

174 A:
2. *Columbian Centinel* journalist Benjamin Russell used the term after a July 1817 visit to Boston by the president.

175 Q:

Harriet Tubman and John Parker were prominent conductors in what famous railroad?

176 Q:

What inventor wrote, "What hath God wrought?"

1. Abner Doubleday
2. Samuel Morse
3. Steve Jobs
4. Thomas Edison
5. Rube Goldberg

177 Q:

Did the Fugitive Slave Act protect the rights of slaves who had escaped to free states?

178 Q:

Dred Scott was born a slave and lived only a few months as a free man. What is his tragic claim to fame?

175 A: The so-called Underground Railroad assisted thousands of fugitive slaves in escaping to Canada and free Northern states in the years before the Civil War.

176 A:
2. For the first message sent on the Baltimore–Washington telegraph line, Morse borrowed this phrase from the Old Testament Book of Numbers. Contrary to popular belief, this 1844 message was not the first successful telegraphed missive. As early as 1838, Morse had delivered another message ("Attention the universe, by kingdom's right wheel") over a distance of two miles.

177 A: On the contrary, the 1850 bill asserted that wherever they were in the U.S., runaway slaves were property, not people. The controversial law that opponents dubbed "the Bloodhound Act" even instituted fines for those who aided the freed slaves and gave cash rewards to those who aided in their capture.

178 A: After this Virginia-born slave offered to buy his family's freedom from his widow owner and was refused, he took his case to court in 1846. It took a full decade for the case to snake its way up to the Supreme Court, but when it did, *Scott v. Sandford* became one of the most significant court decisions in American history.

179 Q:

In the *Scott v. Sandford* case, there were claims of political tampering. On what grounds were they based?

180 Q:

What made this decision about a single enslaved black family so important for our entire country?

181 Q:

When did the Antebellum Era occur?

1. 1776–1800
2. 1800–1830
3. 1830–1860
4. 1860–1890

179 A: Incoming president James Buchanan foolishly believed that a high court decision could enable him to put the entire slavery question behind him before he entered office. After the Supreme Court arguments were heard, but before the decision was handed down, he contacted at least two justices to further his purpose. Even by the lenient standards of the day, this was an improper intrusion. Nevertheless, at first, Buchanan thought he had gotten his wish: The high court made its very decisive ruling only two days after his inauguration.

180 A: Scott lost the case, but sympathizers bought his family's freedom. For the nation, however, the court's rulings had grim ramifications. Not only did the 1857 Dred Scott decision stipulate that no person of African descent had any standing to sue in a federal court, it also argued that the federal government had no power to regulate slavery in U.S. territories created since the country was formed. As Northerners viewed it, this would lead inevitably to a country completely dominated by the slaveholding South.

181 A:
3. True to its Latin etymology, the Antebellum Era marks the time before the war; in this case, the American Civil War.

182 Q:

Who was Tabitha Babbitt?

1. one of America's first professional actresses
2. a Continental spy and smuggler during the Revolutionary War
3. an inventor of a circular saw and false teeth
4. the only woman on the Lewis and Clark Expedition
5. a nurse who established one of Philadelphia's first hospitals

183 Q:

How many political contests did Abraham Lincoln lose before he became president?

184 Q:

When the first Confederate salvos began landing on Fort Sumter, the question arose, "Who would lead the Union forces?" The obvious answer was Lieutenant General Winfield Scott, the commanding officer of the U.S. Army and the man considered by many to be the ablest commander in U.S. military history. But he declined the honor. Why?

182 A:
3. Had Tabitha Babbitt (1784–c.1853) not been a Shaker, she might have cashed in on her inventions of a circular saw, an efficient spinning wheel with a double spinning-head, and a method of cutting multiple nails for construction. At the time of her death, she was working on models of false teeth. Because of her religious beliefs, she never patented any of these innovations.

183 A: Several. Among his losses: the 1832 race for Illinois House of Representatives; an 1838 effort to become speaker in the Illinois state legislature; an 1840 attempt to become a state elector; the 1844 Whig Party nomination for the U.S. House of Representatives; the 1849 General Land Office appointment; the 1854 and 1856 Senate elections; the 1856 Republican vice-presidential nomination; and the 1858 U.S. Senate election.

184 A: At the outbreak of the Civil War, Scott was seventy-four years old and hardly capable of leading an army in the field: By then he weighed more than 300 pounds, and it was said that no horse could him support him.

185 Q:
In his stead, Scott offered the command to his most promising officer, but that young colonel declined. Who was the soldier who refused?

186 Q:
One West Point graduate led a whole nation against the United States. Can you name him?

187 Q:
Which of the original thirteen states seceded from the Union?

188 Q:
Name the other seven states that joined the Confederacy.

189 Q:
How did Confederate general "Stonewall" Jackson earn his nickname?

190 Q:
Which Civil War general popularized a new men's hairstyle?

191 Q:
According to some of the general's military critics, why did the slang term change?

185 A: Robert E. Lee turned down the offer in April 1861 on the same day that the Commonwealth of Virginia joined the Confederacy. Colonel Lee agreed to lead the troops of his home state.

186 A: Jefferson Davis, the only president of the Confederacy, graduated from the United States Military Academy in 1828.

187 A: Georgia, South Carolina, Virginia, and North Carolina.

188 A: Mississippi, Florida, Alabama, Louisiana, Texas, Arkansas, and Tennessee.

189 A: General Thomas Jonathan Jackson, also a West Point graduate, won his nickname at the First Battle of Bull Run the hard way: by holding his ground.

190 A: Union general Ambrose E. Burnside earned a niche in history for his mutton chops, which were first called "burnsides," but then became known as "sideburns." He too was a West Point graduate.

191 A: They said that "burnsides" became "sideburns" because the inept general always did everything backwards.

192 Q:
General George McClellan angered leaders, including President Lincoln, with his indecisiveness, but on one occasion at least, he aggressively pursued the Confederate army. What inspired his sudden infusion of courage before the Battle of Antietam?

193 Q:
In what slave-holding state was Sojourner Truth born?

194 Q:
What was Sojourner Truth's given name?

195 Q:
Which of the following Civil War generals did *not* publish memoirs after the war?

1. Edward Porter Alexander
2. Thomas Jonathan Jackson
3. William T. Sherman
4. George B. McClellan
5. Joseph E. Johnston

196 Q:
On whose estate was Arlington National Cemetery founded?

192 A: Not long before the battle, two Union soldiers discovered a detailed copy of Robert E. Lee's Maryland campaign wrapped in three cigars. Even then, McClellan vacillated for a full eighteen hours before making his move. (History does not tell us who smoked the cigars.)

193 A: New York. She was born into slavery c.1797; New York State did not abolish slavery until 1827.

194 A: Isabella Baumfree. She adopted her memorable name on June 1st, 1843, as she began her journey to preach for the abolition of slavery.

195 A:
2. "Stonewall" Jackson was injured during the Battle of Chancellorsville and died shortly later on May 10, 1863.

196 A: Robert E. Lee's. After Lee assumed his Confederate command, his family fled the Virginia estate. When his wife was unable to return to pay the property taxes, the land was seized and the federal government acquired it at auction. After the war, the Lees spent years trying to regain their beloved home but to no avail; the burial of war dead had rendered their estate uninhabitable.

197 Q:
What else was built at the Arlington estate during the Civil War?

198 Q:
In November 2013, a Harrisburg, Pennsylvania, newspaper issued a somewhat tardy retraction. What was their offense and how did they make amends?

199 Q:
Dr. Richard Mudd, who died in 2002, spent seven decades trying to clear the name of Dr. Samuel Mudd, his grandfather. Who was the older Dr. Mudd, and for what crime was he convicted?

200 Q:
When was the Louisiana Purchase transacted?

1. 1781
2. 1846
3. 1791
4. 1803
5. 1814

197 A: Freedman's Village. Part of the estate was converted into a town for freed slaves. Over a thousand freed slaves lived and worked there until they were evicted in 1888 so the land could be rededicated as a military installation.

198 A: "Seven score and ten years ago," the *Patriot-News* retraction reads, "the forefathers of this media institution brought forth to its audience a judgment so flawed, so tainted by hubris, so lacking in the perspective history would bring that it cannot remain unaddressed in our archives." The editor was apologizing for the paper's dismissal of "silly remarks of the president" and its hopes that "the veil of oblivion shall be dropped over" Abraham Lincoln's Gettysburg speech.

199 A: This Maryland physician was one of eight people convicted of conspiracy in the assassination of President Abraham Lincoln. Soon after the assassination, Mudd set John Wilkes Booth's broken leg and allowed him to rest in his home for several hours. An early lie to investigators and the testimony of four slaves helped ensure his conviction; only one vote saved him from execution. In 1869, he was pardoned from his life sentence because of his medical work stemming from a yellow fever epidemic at the prison.

200 A:
4. The treaty was signed in Paris on April 30, 1803.

201 Q:

How much did the Louisiana Purchase cost?

1. $10 million
2. $15 million
3. $20 million
4. $25 million
5. $30 million

202 Q:

How much is that per acre?

1. 3 cents
2. 8 cents
3. 12 cents
4. 9 cents
5. 18 cents

203 Q:

The Louisiana Purchase included all the land in which of the following states?

1. Arkansas
2. Louisiana
3. Iowa
4. Missouri
5. Oklahoma

201 A:

2. The purchase was, in fact, a steal: The American negotiators in Paris had been willing to pay $10 million for New Orleans and its environs alone, so they were dumbfounded by the French offer. U.S. diplomat Robert R. Livingston had not been authorized to agree to a larger sum, but he was so certain that Washington leaders would welcome the agreement that he accepted it on the spot.

202 A:

1. Even in 2013 dollars, that would be less than forty-four cents an acre.

203 A:

1, 3, 4, and 5. Not all of Louisiana was included in the sale. All or parts of fifteen states and two Canadian provinces were transferred in the purchase.

204 Q:
What was Seward's Folly?

205 Q:
How many square miles were acquired by the U.S. in the Louisiana Purchase?

1. 529,500
2. 581,000
3. 673,606
4. 727,580
5. 828,000

206 Q:
By comparison, approximately how large were the original thirteen colonies?

1. 220,000 square miles
2. 370,000 square miles
3. 550,000 square miles
4. 95,000 square miles
5. 150,000 square miles

204 A: When the United States bought Alaska from Russia in 1867 for $7.2 million, critics scoffed, calling the purchase Seward's Folly, after chief American negotiator William Seward. After an all-night session in July, the former Lincoln cabinet member had agreed to pay the supposedly ridiculous sum of two cents per acre for this mineral-rich land.

205 A:
5. That is an area 120,000 square miles larger than the entire country of Mexico.

206 A:
2. Thus, less than half the size of land acquired in the Louisiana Purchase.

207 Q:

Listed below are the U.S.'s five biggest territorial acquisitions after the Louisiana Purchase. Put them in descending order of size and match them with their date of acquisition.

1.	Mexican Cession	a.	1845
2.	Philippine Islands	b.	1867
3.	Texas	c.	1848
4.	Alaska	d.	1898
5.	Oregon	e.	1846

208 Q:

Which of the following states was not one of the Confederate States of America: Alabama, Arkansas, Florida, Georgia, Kentucky, Louisiana, Mississippi, North Carolina, South Carolina, Tennessee, Texas, and Virginia?

209 Q:

When the Civil War began in 1861, approximately how many blacks were enslaved?

1. 500,000
2. 2 million
3. 3 million
4. 4 million
5. 6 million

207 A:
4 and b;
1 and c;
3 and a;
5 and e;
2 and d.

208 A: Kentucky. Although officially a Union state, Kentucky was deeply divided during the Civil War.

209 A:
4. Since 1830, the slave population of the U.S. had nearly doubled. Before Emancipation, only about 11 percent of African-Americans were free.

210 Q:

When President Abraham Lincoln first met this author, he was reported to have said, "So you're the little woman who wrote the book that made this great war!" Who was the quiet minister's daughter who caused such a national ruckus?

211 Q:

In November 1864, President Lincoln wrote a letter to a woman that became uncommonly famous. Who was its recipient?

1. widow Ellen Pease
2. nurse Clara Barton
3. mother Lydia Bixby
4. actress Laura Keene
5. nurse Dorothea Dix

212 Q:

In which state were the most Civil War battles fought?

1. Tennessee
2. Pennsylvania
3. Mississippi
4. Virginia
5. Maryland

210 A: Harriet Beecher Stowe. Her 1852 anti-slavery novel *Uncle Tom's Cabin* solidified Northern hostility toward the slave-owners of the South.

211 A:

3. It is not surprising that a letter from the president to a mother of "five sons who had died gloriously in the field of battle" would be frequently reprinted and quoted in the wake of the bloody Civil War. Unfortunately, we now know several things that diminish its power: Apparently, three Bixby boys long survived the war. Even worse, Mrs. Bixby herself was a Confederate sympathizer who was also reputed to be a madam. It is said that she destroyed the letter soon after reading it.

212 A:

4. Over 60 percent of the battles fought during the War Between the States took place in the Commonwealth of Virginia.

213 Q:
Who did Mark Twain accuse of causing the Civil War?

214 Q:
At the end of the Civil War, African-Americans formed what percentage of the Union Army?

1. 2 percent
2. 3 percent
3. 5 percent
4. 10 percent
5. 20 percent

215 Q:
Why did Ulysses S. Grant write an autobiography?

216 Q:
Who was his publisher?

217 Q:
Was the book a success and was Grant's widow well served?

213 A: Sir Walter Scott. In his *Life on the Mississippi*, Twain blamed Scott and his novels like *Ivanhoe* for nurturing Southerners' love of rank and caste and their preoccupation with sham chivalry that sowed the seeds of war.

214 A:
4. Although African-Americans comprised only 1 percent of the population of the North, they formed 10 percent of the Union army. Many of these soldiers were freed or escaped slaves from the border states and the South.

215 A: Besides the reasons usually shared by presidents and generals, Grant had an extra incentive to write his memoirs: He was dying. In 1884, he received news that he had throat cancer, an almost certain death sentence in those days. He realized that he needed to leave a suitable inheritance for his wife. In a race against time, he began writing his autobiography. He won the race, but just barely: He finished the book just a few days before he died in July of the following year.

216 A: His friend Mark Twain. The famed author, not always wise in business decisions, promised a hefty royalty.

217 A: Yes and yes. Though written in urgent haste, the two-volume autobiography, which was published in 1886, is still regarded as one of the finest presidential memoirs and has never fallen out of print. As for his widow Julia and their family, they received approximately $450,000 in royalties, the equivalent of $10 million in current dollars.

218 Q:

Who made the 1848 discovery that launched the California gold rush?

1. James Marshall
2. "Klondike Bill" Gibbs
3. John Sutter
4. Bruce Sutter
5. Henry Philip Hope

219 Q:

When was gold first discovered in the Yukon?

218 A:

1. The name of John Sutter will be linked forever with the California gold rush, but it was his trusted employee James Marshall who made the lucky find. The discovery of gold on Sutter's mill settlement didn't make him rich; it bankrupted him. Sutter's property was overrun by hungry prospectors, and his mill was ruined. The German-born immigrant spent the remainder of his life attempting to recoup his devastating losses. He never did. (Marshall died almost destitute, despite receiving a California pension in honor of his historic discovery.)

219 A: On August 17, 1896, American George Carmack and two quaintly nicknamed associates ("Skookum Jim" Mason and "Tagish Charlie" Dawson) uncovered gold nuggets in Rabbit Creek, which quickly became known as Bonanza Creek. After news of that fortuitous find spread, would-be prospectors flocked to the region and the Klondike Gold Rush was on. Only about 10 percent of the 40,000 adventurers, however, struck gold.

Identify the Riot

220 Q:

Thousands of New Yorkers gather outside a Manhattan opera house to protest the appearance of a British Shakespearean actor instead of an American favorite. After the mob attempts to storm the theater, troops are called in. In the ensuing mayhem, twenty-three people die.

221 Q:

A mob of more than 500 men roars into Los Angeles's Chinatown, purportedly to avenge the death of a Caucasian killed in the crossfire of a gunfight between two Chinese. Whatever its original cause or causes, the riot degenerates into a massacre. Eighteen Chinese are lynched.

222 Q:

Five Points gangs, including the Bowery Boys, join battle in a protracted lower Manhattan street brawl, eventually leaving more than a hundred rioters dead.

220 A: The Astor Place Riot of 1849.

221 A: The Chinese Massacre of 1871.

222 A: The Dead Rabbit Riot of 1857. This extended melee began on the Fourth of July in 1857. Sporadic fighting continued for the next week and might have escalated further without the presence of the police.

Identify the Riot (cntd.)

223 Q:

A routine arrest for drunken driving escalates into six deadly days of ghetto riots in Los Angeles. Thirty-four people perish.

224 Q:

In three days of near anarchy, tens of thousands of draft protesters destroy buildings, attack African-American pedestrians, and fight police and soldiers. Over a thousand men and women are injured or killed.

225 Q:

Widespread fighting occurs between white marines and sailors stationed in World War II–era Los Angeles and young Mexican-Americans who favored a distinctive style of dress.

223 A: The Watts Riots of 1965.

224 A: The New York Draft Riots of 1863.

225 A: The Zoot Suit Riots of 1943. These racial riots sparked similar attacks against Latinos in Chicago, Detroit, Philadelphia, New York, Oakland, San Diego, and other cities.

226 Q:

Who set fire to Richmond?

1. No one knows. Theories about the conflagration continue to circulate.
2. A stagehand at the Richmond Theatre accidentally lit a candle near a curtain and the flames spread far beyond the building.
3. Rampaging Union troops set blazes around the city after Confederate troops had fled in April 1865.
4. After the fall of Petersburg, Virginia, retreating Confederate troops were ordered to destroy bridges, the armory, and warehouses.

227 Q:

When did the Emancipation Proclamation go into effect?

1. 1861
2. 1863
3. 1865
4. 1866
5. 1873

226 A:

4. The Confederate military leaders had not intended to destroy the largely unoccupied city, but winds and the absence of a truly functioning fire department soon left the Southern capital both abandoned and ruined.

227 A:

2. The Emancipation Proclamation, which freed the slaves in the ten states still in rebellion, became law by Abraham Lincoln's executive order on January 1, 1863.

228 Q:

Match the Civil War battle with its description.

1. Lee's first push into the North resulted in a Northern victory and Southern bloodbath.
2. The first major battle of the conflict ended with a rout of Union troops—and spectators.
3. The decisive three-day battle in 1863 concluded with Lee's dramatic withdrawal.
4. The last Confederate stronghold on the Mississippi fell on Independence Day, 1863.

a. Gettysburg
b. Bull Run
c. Vicksburg
d. Antietam

229 Q:

What famous event occurred at Seneca Falls?

230 Q:

Who argued for the right to vote at the convention?

231 Q:

Who wore the first "bloomers"?

232 Q:

After being roundly ridiculed, why was the bloomer craze revived in the 1890s?

228 A:
1 and **d**;
2 and **b**;
3 and **a**;
4 and **c**.

229 A: The Seneca Falls Convention held July 19–20, 1848, was the first women's rights assembly in the country.

230 A: Frederick Douglass, the only African-American present, debated in favor of women's suffrage. The result? A large majority of attendees voted to include the resolution in the Declaration of Sentiments.

231 A: It was not Amelia Bloomer, but Elizabeth Smith Miller who first sported the women's trousers at Seneca Falls in 1851. Bloomer popularized the fashion in her women's reform journal, *The Lily*.

232 A: Bicycles. Wearing bloomers was the only way to get around town on the latest transportation fad.

233 Q:
The first female candidate for president of the United States was Victoria Woodhull in 1872, but why do many question the legality of her candidacy?

234 Q:
Woodhull was a very wealthy woman when she ran for office. How did she make her money?

235 Q:
Who was Mary Todd Lincoln's dressmaker?

236 Q:
What did Mrs. Lincoln do with her dresses?

237 Q:
What state was the first to recognize women's right to vote? In what year did that historic event occur?

1. Wyoming
2. Massachusetts
3. Montana
4. New York
5. Vermont

233 A: Woodhull would have been younger than the constitutionally mandated minimum age of thirty-five.

234 A: She and her sister made a fortune on Wall Street when they became the first women stockbrokers in 1870. The sisters had previously worked as clairvoyants for Cornelius Vanderbilt, who was so impressed by their predictions that he provided them with financial backing for their own firm.

235 A: Elizabeth Hobbs Keckley. A former slave, she became the First Lady's personal dresser, sole designer, and confidante during the Lincoln presidency. Keckley wrote a memoir of her years at the White House called *Behind the Scenes*, but was widely criticized for violating Mary Todd's privacy.

236 A: Eventually she sold most of them to pay her ever-mounting debts. After her husband was assassinated, Mary was grief- and poverty-stricken. With no income and her White House credit bill coming due, she sold much of her lavish wardrobe through dealers; however, her Keckley inauguration gown can still be seen in the Smithsonian.

237 A:
1. When Wyoming achieved statehood in 1890, it became the first state to endorse female suffrage. By that time, female residents of the state had been voting for over two decades. Wyoming Territory legalized women's right to vote in 1869.

238 Q:

Who was the first American woman to win the Nobel Peace Prize?

239 Q:

In 1840, how many buffalo roamed the Great Plains?

1. 2 million
2. 20 million
3. 40 million
4. 60 million
5. 80 million

240 Q:

By 1880, how many wild buffalo still roamed the American prairies?

1. 1 million
2. 2 million
3. 5 million
4. 10 million
5. 12 million

241 Q:

To what or whom do we owe the term "private eye"?

238 A: Jane Addams in 1931. In addition to being a pioneering social reformer, she helped found the women's international peace movement at the start of World War I.

239 A: 3 and 4 are credible estimates. One early explorer described a sixty-square-mile area as "as far as we could see . . . a seemingly solid mass of buffaloes."

240 A:
1. In just a single three-year period in the early 1870s, hide hunters and sportsmen shooting from moving trains killed eight million buffalo, turning the Great Plains into a slaughterhouse of rotting corpses. By 1900, there were fewer than 1,500 bison left.

241 A: The logo of the famous Pinkerton investigating agency was a picture of a wide-open eye and the words, "WE NEVER SLEEP." From that indelible image came a nickname that stuck.

242 Q:
The Molly Maguires were a nineteenth-century
organization formed in Ireland. Why are they still
controversial today in the United States?

243 Q:
"You furnish the pictures and I'll furnish the war" was
the legendary command of a famous newspaper editor
and yellow journalist. Who was he and to whom did he
give his order?

1. Joseph Pulitzer to illustrator Walter Crane
2. Harold Ross to an unnamed photographer
3. William Randolph Hearst to editorial cartoonist
   Thomas Nast
4. William Randolph Hearst to illustrator Frederic
   Remington

244 Q:
Henry Clay Frick was a very rich industrialist, but he
was also a very lucky man. Aside from his immense
wealth, what else did he have to be grateful for?

242 A: The Mollies were a secret society, and much of their notoriety relates to the difficulty of substantiating or disproving claims about them. In fact, some historians deny that the group even formally existed in the U.S., while others claim that they were responsible for much of the murder, mayhem, and terrorism in the coal-mining region of Pennsylvania during the late nineteenth century. For ten accused members, however, those questions became purely academic: They were executed by hanging in June 1877.

243 A:
4. According to an apocryphal story, media mogul William Randolph Hearst wired this response to artist Frederic Remington's request to return from Cuba, where there was no war to cover. Hearst received his warfare wish: The Spanish-American War began in April 1898.

244 A: In July 1892, anarchist Alexander Berkman attempted to assassinate Frick in revenge for the nine striking steelworkers killed by private security forces that the factory owner had hired. Berkman succeeded in shooting him twice in the neck and stabbing him four times, but Frick somehow survived and was back to work within a week. His good fortune didn't stop there: He and his wife had tickets booked aboard the doomed *Titanic*, but her sprained ankle caused them to forgo the trip.

245 Q:
When was the Gilded Age?

1. 1800–1820
2. 1820–1845
3. 1830–1861
4. 1865–1875
5. 1870–1900

246 Q:
Who named the Gilded Age?

1. Charles Dudley Warner
2. Stanford White
3. Andrew Carnegie
4. Mark Twain
5. John Jacob Astor

247 Q:
During one presidential campaign, a major party candidate was victimized by opponents' chants of "Ma, ma, where's my pa?" Who was the White House aspirant and why the ruckus?

245 A:
5. Not surprisingly, this period of enormous industrial growth and widening economic inequality generated both great opulence and fervent social discord.

246 A:
1 and 4. Although the term now carries connotations of elegance and good taste, authors Mark Twain and Charles Dudley Warner clearly intended it as a sign of derision. They adapted the name of their 1873 novel *The Gilded Age: A Story of Today* from a quotation from Shakespeare's *King John*: "To gild refined gold, to paint the lily . . . is wasteful and ridiculous excess." Gilding, in this sense, is to apply only a thin layer of gold over baser metals.

247 A: In late July 1884, just weeks after the Democratic convention had named him their presidential candidate, Grover Cleveland was accused by a Buffalo newspaper of fathering a baby with widow Maria Crofts Halpin. Later, Cleveland, a bachelor, freely admitted that he had provided financial aid for the child, but said that he had no idea whether he was indeed the father. Of course, to the opposition, that made little matter. Cleveland supporters, however, had the final word, with a triumphant answering refrain of "Gone to the White House, ha, ha, ha!"

248 Q:
In the same 1884 campaign, the opposing candidate
fell victim to backlash over a statement that one of his
supporters made. Who was he and what was the slogan
that brought him down?

249 Q:
In January 1919, Boston experienced a major condiment
disaster. What caused this catastrophe and how serious
was it?

250 Q:
What percentage of Americans can trace their ancestry
to the immigrants who first arrived at Ellis Island?

248 A: Republican presidential candidate James Blaine had hoped that having a Roman Catholic mother might help him in swing states including New York, but those hopes were dashed in the last weeks of the campaign after Empire State minister Samuel D. Burchard had denounced the Democrats as the party of "Rum, Romanism, and Rebellion." ("Romanism" was a pejorative term for supposedly alien Catholics.)

249 A: The Great Boston Molasses Flood was no laughing matter. The explosion of a giant steel tank containing twenty-six million pounds of the viscous liquid unleashed a thirty-five-mile-an-hour wave, engulfing hundreds of Bostonians, drowning horses, knocking down elevated tracks, and destroying homes and businesses. Twenty-one people died and more than 150 were injured. As for the cause, anarchists were blamed, but the culprit was really shoddy construction work.

250 A: Over 100 million Americans, or one-third of our population, have a forebear who first entered the U.S. through our country's busiest immigration reception center from 1892 to 1954. During those years, more than twelve million newcomers were processed by the U.S. Department of Immigration.

251 Q:

The Statue of Liberty was a gift from what country in what year?

1. France in 1875
2. England in 1881
3. France in 1886
4. Canada in 1874

252 Q:

Which New York City police commissioner later became president?

253 Q:

The Yellow Kid is regarded as the forerunner of modern comic strips. When did it first appear?

254 Q:

The Yellow Kid comic strip has also been credited with providing the name for what journalistic trend?

251 A:
1 and 3. The French first announced the gift of a statue entitled "Liberty Enlightening the World" in 1875 in preparation for the following year's Centennial Exhibition in Philadelphia, but it wasn't until October 1886 that the gift was formally accepted by President Grover Cleveland.

252 A: Theodore Roosevelt remembered his two-year stint (1895–1897) as the city's police commissioner with some regret. For one thing, his resolute attempts to enforce the state's Sunday closing laws on New York's 12,000 to 15,000 bars made him the most unpopular man in the great metropolis. Drinking three million fewer glasses of beer might, however, have slimmed the waistlines of countless ungrateful New Yorkers.

253 A: Richard F. Outcault created the Yellow Kid character in his 1895 *New York World* strip *Hogan's Alley*. However, it wasn't until William Randolph Hearst had lured the popular sketch artist to his *New York Journal* that the Kid was honored with his own comic strip name.

254 A: Many media historians believe that the term "yellow journalism" derived from the tabloid newspaper circulation wars first epitomized by the Hearst–Pulitzer struggle for publication rights to *The Yellow Kid*. The term became a catchphrase for the sensationalistic stories and pictures that these papers featured.

255 Q:
One New York newspaper responded to the competition of these scandal-sodden tabloids with a front-page affirmation. What was this pointed motto and who made it?

256 Q:
With juicy details like a headless, dismembered corpse; a love triangle; and an abortionist killer, one 1897 murder mystery riveted New York City and re-stoked the tabloid war. What was the name of the real-life case that some have called the murder of the century?

257 Q:
Of the 5,642 Americans killed during the Spanish-American War, how many died in battle?

1. 3,872
2. 2,642
3. 2,497
4. 1,097
5. 379

258 Q:
Did William McKinley enjoy his first automobile ride?

255 A: "ALL THE NEWS THAT'S FIT TO PRINT." In February 1897, publisher Adolph Ochs moved this editorial page banner to the front page of his *New York Times*, where it has remained ever since.

256 A: The Guldensuppe case. What began with the July discovery of a mutilated torso became a race for resolution that frequently left police and prosecutors far behind the competing tabloid newsmen. In other situations, the violent demise of working-class masseur Willie Guldensuppe would have gone mostly unnoticed, but Hearst's *New York Journal* and Pulitzer's *New York World* transformed the story into a circulation booster that left all other newspapers in the dust. At one stage, a huge Hearst headline blared: "MURDER MYSTERY SOLVED BY THE JOURNAL. MRS. NACK, MURDERESS!" After the court cases ended with one confession and one execution, the newspapers rested until Hearst reopened with even stronger salvos for a Cuban war.

257 A:
5. Disease, not gunfire, was the big killer of this war.

258 A: Probably not. He had other things on his mind: He had just been shot twice by an assassin. The electric-powered ambulance that drove him to the hospital on September 6, 1901, might have been a rarity in its time, but the president was laboring under painful distractions.

259 Q:
What caused McKinley's death?

260 Q:
Who was Leon Czolgosz and what was his claim to fame or infamy?

261 Q:
Who did he identify as his inspirations?

262 Q:
When did Mrs. O'Leary's cow cause the Chicago Fire?

259 A: The simple answer, of course, is the two bullets that his assassin shot into his abdomen. But the twenty-fifth president survived for more than a week after the shooting. It was the gangrene emanating from the bullet wounds that spread through his bloodstream and killed him.

260 A: Czolgosz was the unemployed Michigan factory worker who murdered President William McKinley. Reclusive, furtive, and erratic, he claimed to be an anarchist, but didn't mesh well with other radicals. In fact, the *Free Society* newspaper identified him as a probable spy.

261 A: Emma Goldman and Alexander Berkman. Czolgosz had read works by both Russian-born anarchists and attended at least one lecture by Goldman, after which he was so impressed that he had twice pursued her for reading suggestions. Ultimately, she had no reason to be flattered: Soon after the assassination, she was arrested and subjected to intense interrogation about her supposed complicity. Nevertheless, almost alone among her countrymen, she defended the mentally ill assassin as "supersensitive."

262 A: The great Windy City conflagration began on October 8, 1871, but to this day it is unclear how it started. Mrs. O'Leary's bovine, however, became the fall guy (cow). The story that portrayed her as an arsonist later proved to be a concoction of an enterprising reporter intent on creating a memorable account.

263 Q:

Who coined the term "muckraker"?

1. William Randolph Hearst
2. Upton Sinclair
3. Theodore Roosevelt
4. Charles Edward Russell

264 Q:

Identify the muckraker:

1. His gut-wrenching novel *The Jungle* won public support for the Meat Inspection Act and the Pure Food and Drug Act.
2. Her history of Standard Oil exposed the monopolistic practices of the great American trust.
3. His articles, collected in *The Shame of the Cities*, revealed the degrading conditions of urban existence.
4. His satirical cartoons targeted corrupt Tammany bosses.

265 Q:

When was the first running of the Kentucky Derby?

266 Q:

What famous historical name was associated with this event?

263 A:
3. Roosevelt borrowed a name from *Pilgrim's Progress* to describe reporters who searched for stories about the seamy side of life in progressive America.

264 A:
1. Upton Sinclair.
2. Ida Tarbell.
3. Lincoln Steffens.
4. Thomas Nast.

265 A: Louisville's first Derby day was on May 17, 1875.

266 A: The Kentucky Derby was organized by Colonel Meriwether Lewis Clark Jr., the grandson of Meriwether Lewis of the Lewis and Clark Expedition.

267 Q:
What American became the prime minister of Israel?

268 Q:
What American-born man became prime minister and president of Ireland?

269 Q:
What was the first U.S. national park and when did it open?

270 Q:
Who fought at the Battle of Wounded Knee on December 29, 1890?

271 Q:
When did the Great San Francisco Earthquake strike?

272 Q:
What educational first did W. E. B. Du Bois attain?

267 A: Golda Meir. Israel's first female prime minister was born in Czarist Russia, but grew up in Milwaukee after her family emigrated to the U.S. in 1906.

268 A: Éamon de Valera was the first president of the Irish Republic (1921–1922), but this son of Irish and Cuban immigrant parents was born in New York City.

269 A: Yosemite National Park, which first welcomed visitors on March 1, 1872.

270 A: This one-sided battle was the last significant conflict fought between Native Americans and U.S. troops. Over 200 Sioux, led by Chief Big Foot, were massacred at South Dakota's Wounded Knee Creek by the United States Seventh Cavalry.

271 A: On April 18, 1906, San Francisco suffered its worst seismic upheaval. This quake and the fires and aftershocks that followed, left 503 dead and caused $350 million in damages. Approximately 80 percent of the city was destroyed.

272 A: When he received his doctorate in 1895, William Edward Burghardt Du Bois became the first African-American to receive a Ph.D. from Harvard.

273 Q:

Who was the first scientist to discover the many uses of peanuts, including peanut butter?

274 Q:

Who were the "Buffalo Soldiers"?

275 Q:

Who was the first black major league player?

276 Q:

Who was the first black Supreme Court justice?

273 A: George Washington Carver was born a slave and was separated from his family, but he never allowed personal tragedies to slow his efforts to improve life for others. Over several decades, he developed hundreds of uses for peanuts, sweet potatoes, and soybeans, as well as a new type of cotton known as Carver's hybrid.

274 A: After the Civil War, the U.S. created fighting units of African-American soldiers. They played an important role in the history of the American West. In addition to combat duties, they explored and mapped much of the Southwest, strung telegraph lines, built frontier outposts, and protected settlers from attacks. The Cheyenne named them the "buffalo soldiers."

275 A: Jackie Robinson deserves great praise for putting himself on the line to break the modern baseball color barrier in 1947, when the future Hall of Famer joined the Brooklyn Dodgers. A less well-known pathfinder is Moses Fleetwood "Fleet" Walker: In 1884, this African-American catcher played one season in the American Association, which was then a major league. Like Robinson, he battled with vicious racial prejudice during his career.

276 A: Thurgood Marshall, who was appointed by President Lyndon B. Johnson to the nation's highest court in 1967.

277 Q:

Can you name the first African-American to win the Nobel Peace Prize?

278 Q:

Who was the first African-American to have his own television show? How did it fare?

279 Q:

Something happened in 1898 that no resident in New York City's five boroughs could ignore. What was it?

280 Q:

When did New York City become the most populous city in the world?

1. 1885
2. 1895
3. 1915
4. 1925
5. 1935

277 A: Ralph Bunche, who received the vaunted prize in 1950 for his work as a mediator in Palestine, while serving as the director of the United Nations Division of Trusteeship. Reverend Martin Luther King, who won the Peace Prize in 1964, remains the youngest African-American Peace Prize laureate.

278 A: Nat "King" Cole. His variety TV show made history when it debuted in late 1956. Despite Cole's own remarkable talent and outstanding guests including Ella Fitzgerald, Frankie Laine, Harry Belafonte, Eartha Kitt, and Peggy Lee, the show could not find a national sponsor. When it folded just one year later, Cole sadly quipped, "Madison Avenue is afraid of the dark."

279 A: For the first time, Manhattan, Brooklyn, the Bronx, Queens, and Staten Island became one municipality.

280 A:
4. With urban populations burgeoning around the globe, Gotham soon lost that distinction. Today it no longer rates even among the top ten world cities in population, even though it has more than twice as many inhabitants as any other U.S. city.

281 Q:

When was the Panama Canal opened?

1. 1896
2. 1899
3. 1903
4. 1906
5. 1914

282 Q:

At the wedding between Franklin Delano Roosevelt and Eleanor Roosevelt, who gave the bride away?

283 Q:

Of which U.S. president did historian Jill Lepore write, "No other American has ever gone from private life to the White House in so short a time, and . . . with so unlikely a resume. He had never fought in a war. He had never served in any legislature. He had never had success as a businessman. Aside from his academic appointments, his offices were imaginary."

284 Q:

What did newbie elected official Woodrow Wilson say about hard-knock Jersey politics after being elected Garden State governor in 1910?

281 A:
5. After more than thirty years of planning and construction, the Panama Canal finally opened officially on August 15, 1914.

282 A: Her uncle (and former president) Theodore Roosevelt, of course.

283 A: Woodrow Wilson.

284 A: He assured a friend that it was no match for the academic infighting he had encountered at Princeton.

285 Q:
How many garment workers were killed in the Triangle Shirtwaist Factory fire of 1911?

286 Q:
Why did so many die?

287 Q:
Who was Topsy the Elephant and how was she immortalized?

288 Q:
What development in electricity was Thomas Edison targeting with this event?

285 A: One hundred and forty six. Most were immigrant women, seventeen were men, and almost half were teenagers.

286 A: Because the owners had locked the exit doors of this high-rise factory to prevent employee theft, the seamstresses found themselves trapped when a fire broke out on the eighth floor. Many of the young women, with their clothes and hair burning, jumped to their deaths from windows.

287 A: Topsy was a former circus elephant that spent the last years of her life as an attraction at Coney Island's Luna Park. After years of ill treatment, Topsy killed a trainer; as a consequence, she was deemed a threat and sentenced to death. Thomas Edison came up with the idea of executing her via electrocution. In 1903 the event was recorded on film and released to audiences throughout the country as *Electrocuting an Elephant*.

288 A: Alternating current, or AC. Edison's patent for direct current (DC), the established standard for electrical distribution in the U.S., was under threat by the new AC technology developed by George Westinghouse and Nikola Tesla. Edison hoped to discredit the high voltage break-through by demonstrating its inherent danger. Despite Topsy's cinematic demise, AC won out, and Westinghouse Electric went on to be a major competitor to Edison's General Electric.

289 Q:
Who said, "Any customer can have a car painted any color that he wants so long as it is black"?

290 Q:
What was the "Tin Lizzie" and when did it make its first appearance?

291 Q:
In 1914 what did Ford pay his assembly line workers?

292 Q:
When was the Ford Motor Company founded?

293 Q:
When did General Motors celebrate its centennial?

289 A: Henry Ford in 1909. He was referring to the newly manufactured Model T, which was only available in gray, green, blue, and red. Ford's color philosophy was not implemented until 1914 when his factory switched to a quick-drying paint.

290 A: The automobile with the memorable nickname was the Ford Model T. First introduced in October 1908, the "Tin Lizzie" dominated U.S. car sales for the next eighteen years.

291 A: Five dollars per day. Although more than double the prevailing wage, the increase in pay reduced turnover, expanded production, and increased sales: Workers could now afford to buy Model Ts.

292 A: 1903. Henry Ford had been designing, building, and even racing vehicles as early as 1896, but it wasn't until seven years later that he organized and became president of the company that still bears his name. (Two years earlier, he had resigned in a dispute from the Henry Ford Company, a stockholder-held company that carried his name.)

293 A: 2008. Actually, some of the units of the company were older: For example, the Olds Motor Company was founded in 1897. When William Durant organized General Motors in 1908, it included only the Buick Motor Company. In the next two years, it added Olds and Cadillac. By the 1920s, General Motors was the largest car manufacturer on the planet.

294 Q:
When did the last Plymouth roll off the assembly line?

295 Q:
Speaking of assembly lines, who invented them?

296 Q:
Which car was the first to offer air-conditioning?

297 Q:
When was the first car theft?

298 Q:
To whom did the Rev. Frederick Gates say, "Your fortune is rolling up like an avalanche! You must distribute it faster than it grows! If you do not, it will crush you and your children and your children's children!"?

294 A: The last car with the Plymouth marquee was manufactured by Daimler Chrysler (previously the Chrysler Corporation) on June 28, 2001.

295 A: Contrary to popular belief, it was Ransom E. Olds, not Henry Ford. Automobile manufacturer Olds introduced the moving assembly line in 1901. Ford improved this innovation by installing conveyer belts, which speeded up the process significantly.

296 A: Newspapers raved when Packard exhibited a car with an interior cooling system at the Chicago Automobile Show in November 1939. However, the first fully automatic air-conditioned car was the 1964 Cadillac.

297 A: Auto thievery is almost as old as the car itself. The first car pilfery took place in June 1896, when a felonious mechanic drove away with Baron de Zuylen's Peugeot.

298 A: John D. Rockefeller. The Baptist clergyman was the manager of Rockefeller's fortune and his principal philanthropic adviser.

299 Q:

When Rockefeller formed the Standard Oil Company in 1870, how much of the country's oil did it control? By the end of the decade, how much did it control?

300 Q:

When Standard Oil was dissolved by the Sherman Anti-Trust Act in 1911, how much money did Rockefeller lose?

301 Q:

Which of the following oil companies did *not* evolve from the breakup of Standard Oil?

1. Exxon
2. Mobil
3. Chevron
4. Sunoco
5. Amoco

302 Q:

When was the first Woolworth's store opened?

303 Q:

When did Sears, Roebuck and Company begin?

299 A: 10 and 90 percent, respectively.

300 A: None. His shares in the trust doubled, and he became the richest man in the world.

301 A:
4. Standard Oil of New Jersey was called Esso and renamed Exxon; Standard Oil of New York was called Socony and renamed Mobil; Standard Oil of California was called Socal and renamed Chevron; and Standard Oil of Indiana was called Stanolind and renamed Amoco. Sunoco got its start as the People's Natural Gas Company in Pittsburgh.

302 A: Frank W. Woolworth opened the first five-and-dime store in Utica, New York, on February 22, 1879. A chapter closed in retail history when the last Woolworth's store closed in 1997.

303 A: In 1886, just a year after launching in Minneapolis, the R. W. Sears Watch Company moved to Chicago, where they hired a Mr. Roebuck as a watchmaker. Seven years later, Sears, Roebuck and Company was formed. By then, the firm had already begun to issue the first of its famous catalogs.

304 Q:

In what year was Barnes & Noble founded?

305 Q:

Did Elisha Graves Otis invent the elevator?

306 Q:

How long was the Chrysler Building the tallest building in the world?

307 Q:

What was Ives McGaffey's Whirlwind and why did it create such a big stir?

304 A: In 1873, Charles Barnes opened a book business in Wheaton, Illinois. Forty-four years later, his bookseller son formed a bookselling partnership with Gilbert Clifford Noble, thus forming the now famous name.

305 A: No, hoists already existed. It was Otis's 1853 invention of the elevator brake that provided assurance that these high-climbing pods wouldn't plunge—obviously a necessary improvement.

306 A: Eleven months. The famed Art Deco skyscraper completed construction on May 28, 1930, and was the tallest building at 1,046 feet until the Empire State Building passed it with a height of 1,250 feet. Another New York building had an even shorter run as tallest building: 40 Wall Street was finished in April 1930, only to see the Chrysler Building hoist its spire a month later.

307 A: The crank-operated Whirlwind of 1869 was the first American vacuum cleaner. By all accounts, McGaffey's Windy City cleaner was light, compact, and difficult to operate. Home care took a great leap forward with James Spangler's 1907 invention of the first functioning electric vacuum cleaner. The Hoover Company of New Berlin, Ohio, rolled out its first electric Model O in 1908.

308 Q:
Who invented blue jeans?

309 Q:
Did Colgate invent modern American toothpaste?

310 Q:
When was toothpaste first marketed in collapsible tubes?
To what do we owe this invention?

311 Q:
Who invented the windshield wiper?

308 A: No, it was not Levi Strauss. However, the German immigrant does have an important part in the story: It was Nevada tailor Jacob Davis who came up with the idea of placing metal rivets on denim at the points of strain. In 1873, he approached the dry goods merchant with news of his breakthrough. The two patented the process and Levi Strauss began marketing the jeans.

309 A: Not by a long shot. English immigrant William Colgate set up his New York–based starch, soap, and candle business in 1806, but it wasn't until 1873, more than twenty years after the death of the company's founder, that Colgate & Company joined the battle for toothpaste market share. Their first teeth cleaners were sold in jars.

310 A: In 1892, Dr. Washington Sheffield manufactured toothpaste in a collapsible tube. (Before then, toothpaste was sold in jars.) The Connecticut dentist received the idea for his invention from his son's observation that Parisian artists used paint from tubes.

311 A: In 1903, Mary Anderson received a patent for this indispensable invention. Her version cleaned precipitation and debris from the car windshield by use of a handle inside the vehicle. By 1916, windshield wipers were standard issue in American cars.

312 Q:
Who invented the safety pin?

313 Q:
When did the first movie theater open?

314 Q:
According to folklore, who deserves partial credit for the invention?

315 Q:
Were they able to cash in on their movie breakthrough?

312 A: This handy little device was concocted by Walter Hunt of New York, who made the discovery while absent-mindedly twisting a small piece of wire. On April 10, 1849, Hunt patented his safety pin invention, but later sold the patent for a just few hundred dollars. He didn't get rich, but his brainchild has made countless mothers very grateful.

313 A: Richard Hollingshead Jr. opened a drive-in movie theater in Camden, New Jersey, on June 6, 1933. He hoped it would be enough of an attraction to boost sales at his gas station. It was sold out the first night (the first film shown was *Wife Beware*) and for many nights after that.

314 A: Hollingshead's mother was apparently a very plus-sized woman who didn't like the confines of seats at local movie theaters. It was, we are told, through experiments designed to give his mom a car-seat cinematic experience that gave the inventor the inspiration and ideas to become the first drive-in mogul.

315 A: No. This ambitious entrepreneur patented his invention even before his first drive-in opening, but was unable to really benefit from the great boom he started. (At their peak in the late fifties and early sixties, movies were shown at more than 4,000 drive-in venues.) Unfortunately for Hollingshead, his patent afforded him no real protection; in fact, in 1950, it was ruled invalid.

316 Q:
Who invented the zipper?

317 Q:
In what year was the first successful Wright Brothers airplane flight?

318 Q:
Who was the first person to fly over the South Pole?

319 Q:
Who developed the world's first polio vaccine and when was it first tested?

316 A: Chicago engineer Whitcomb Judson patented the first zipper in 1893 and exhibited it at the Chicago World's Fair that year. However, the new invention didn't catch on (so to speak) until B. F. Goodrich put zippers on his product—rubber galoshes. Goodrich also coined the term: Until then, zippers had been known only as "hookless fasteners."

317 A: 1903. In December of that year, Orville Wright piloted the first heavier-than-air, machine-powered flight in the history of the world. Although it lasted only twelve seconds, his 120-foot flight over the sand dunes of Kitty Hawk, North Carolina, immortalized him and brother Wilbur. A later flight that day went a jaw-dropping 852 feet.

318 A: Richard E. Byrd. The American admiral made aviation history when he flew his tri-motor plane over the southern pole in November of 1928.

319 A: Dr. Jonas Salk, the son of Jewish immigrant parents, began testing his vaccine in 1952. Thanks to the Salk vaccine and the subsequent oral vaccine developed by Dr. Albert Sabin, a disease that once afflicted and paralyzed hundreds of thousands worldwide each year has now become a rarity. Neither Salk nor Sabin patented their priceless discoveries.

320 Q:
How many people died in the flu epidemic of 1918–1919?

321 Q:
In what decade did the U.S. welcome the highest number of immigrants?

322 Q:
The corner of East Euclid and East 105th Street is the most famous intersection in Cleveland, Ohio. One day in 1914, it was the site of a history-making event. What happened that day that made it so special?

323 Q:
In addition to that ingenious device, with what other life-saving inventions can this son of a freed slave be credited?

320 A: In the three waves of the 1918–1919 "Spanish Flu," at least twenty million people succumbed worldwide. Indeed, many estimates run as high as thirty million dead. Approximately 28 percent of Americans experienced symptoms, and fatality estimates begin at half a million. Coming on the heels of the First World War (in which ten million perished), the pandemic spread more quickly and widely because of the large troop movements of the time.

321 A: From 2000 to 2010, more than thirteen million new legal and illegal immigrants arrived on our shores. No previous decade can top that figure.

322 A: On that corner on August 5, Garrett Morgan installed the world's first electric traffic signal.

323 A: This master mechanic and experimenter also designed a protective respiratory hood (or gas mask) and a self-extinguishing safety cigarette. He wasn't simply an armchair scientist either: In 1916, he put his own life at risk helping to save survivors of a Lake Erie natural gas explosion.

324 Q:
When were Wheaties invented?

325 Q:
When was the advertising slogan "Wheaties—The Breakfast of Champions" introduced?

326 Q:
When was soda first sold in a can?

327 Q:
Who invented basketball?

328 Q:
Who invented "mintonette" and what is it?

324 A: In 1921, Wheaties were created accidentally when a Minneapolis health clinician spilled some of the bran gruel he was mixing onto a hot stove. The gruel crackled into a crisp flake. Encouraged by its taste, he took his new discovery to officials at the nearby Washburn Crosby Company, where head miller George Cormack tested varieties of wheat before developing the perfect commercial flake. In 1924, the firm introduced the cereal.

325 A: In 1933. The tagline became immediately popular, especially because it meshed well with Wheaties' radio sponsorship of sports events.

326 A: The soda can was first featured locally in 1938 by the Continental Can Company of Mills, Massachusetts. However, it wasn't until RC Cola first distributed soda cans nationally in 1954 that the idea went truly coast-to-coast.

327 A: James Naismith. In 1891, this strong-willed physical education teacher answered a call to create an inexpensive indoor athletic activity for the students at the School for Christian Workers in Springfield, Massachusetts. Hoop enthusiasts have been playing the game ever since.

328 A: YMCA instructor William Morgan created the game of volleyball in 1895 in Holyoke, Massachusetts. Fortunately for all concerned, the name he gave the game quickly vanished from history.

329 Q:

For these famous American trials, match the defendant and key witness:

1. Bruno Richard Hauptmann   a. David Greenglass
2. Alger Hiss   b. Evelyn Nesbit
3. O. J. Simpson   c. Charles Lindbergh
4. Julius and Ethel Rosenberg   d. Whitaker Chambers
5. Harry Thaw   e. Mark Fuhrman

330 Q:

What was "the Monkey Trial"?

1. Actually, it wasn't a real trial at all. It was a newspaper-sponsored courtroom debate about evolution that was staged in North Carolina in 1919.

2. In Pennsylvania, a woman was charged with the death of a stranger who had been mauled by her pet orangutan.

3. A Tennessee schoolteacher was placed on trial for illegally teaching Darwinian principles to his students.

4. In a protracted 2009 appellate court case, parents of a West Virginia high-school student argued that their daughter should be allowed to replace a science course with one consistent with intelligent design.

329 A:
1 and c.
2 and d.
3 and e.
4 and a.
5 and b.

330 A:
3. In the summer of 1925, John T. Scopes, a twenty-four-year-old substitute biology teacher, was put on trial for illegally teaching evolution to high school students. The proceedings, dubbed "the Monkey Trial" by the press, drew national media attention.

331 Q:

Who were the two prominent lawyers involved in the Scopes trial?

1. Lucas Jackson
2. Clarence Darrow
3. William Bell Riley
4. William Jennings Bryan

332 Q:

Which of the following statements is not true about Antonio López de Santa Anna?

1. He was president of Mexico on eleven separate occasions.
2. He played a part in the history of chewing gum.
3. He fathered more than half a dozen illegitimate children.
4. He was the winning general at the Alamo.
5. While living in Staten Island, he attempted to raise an army to retake Mexico City.

331 A:

2 and 4. The stakes for Scopes were relatively small, but his case attracted two major lawyers: Clarence Darrow, regarded by many as the most compelling defense lawyer of his time, and William Jennings Bryan, a three-time presidential candidate. Each had strong motivations for his advocacy: Darrow was a vocal agnostic, and Bryan a devout fundamentalist Christian. The results of the trial were mixed: Scopes was convicted, but given only the minimum fine ($100), which was nullified after a successful appeal.

332 A: Believe it or not, all five statements are true. Most interesting perhaps is his connection to the chronicles of chewing gum: In 1868, while living in exile, he sold some *chicle* to Thomas Adams, a New Jersey inventor who was experimenting with vulcanized rubber. Noticing that Santa Anna, like many other Mexicans, enjoyed chewing on *chicle*, Adams boiled a small batch to create a chewing gum. Later, he flavored it with licorice and marketed the product. In 1871, he introduced the first commercially packed, flavored chewing gum—Black Jack. From this breakthrough, Santa Anna gained not a penny, thus further frustrating his plans to recapture his country.

333 Q:
He was born as either Henry McCarty or William Henry McCarty in New York City, perhaps in 1859. How did this lowly immigrants' son eventually achieve lasting renown?

334 Q:
How many people did he kill?

335 Q:
Who killed him and how old was "The Kid" when he died?

336 Q:
What name did "Billy the Kid" go by during his years of notoriety?

337 Q:
How did Jesse James die?

338 Q:
How many films have been made about Jesse James?

333 A: He became the desperado known as "Billy the Kid."

334 A: According to legend, as many as twenty-one. More reliable estimates set the toll between four and nine.

335 A: Sheriff Pat Garrett shot Billy in a showdown in Fort Sumner, New Mexico, in July 1881. The outlaw did not live to see his twenty-second birthday.

336 A: William H. Bonney. According to biographers, it is possible that Bonney was the surname of his birth father or stepfather.

337 A: On April 3, 1882, Jesse James was standing on a chair, innocently cleaning a dusty picture on the wall when he was shot in the back of the head by reward-seeker Robert Ford. Thereafter, Ford, an outlaw himself, was known as "the dirty coward who shot Mr. Howard"—Howard being Jesse James's last-known alias. For his execution, Ford received only $500. He supplemented that bounty by posing for "he killed Jesse James" photographs at dime museums and reenacting the crime on stage, but for obvious reasons, his act attracted more derision than praise.

338 A: More than two dozen, not counting television productions.

339 Q:

Who fought at the O.K. Corral on October 26, 1881?

340 Q:

What was Doc Holliday before he became a gunfighter?

341 Q:

What was Annie Oakley's birth name?

342 Q:

On her European tour, Annie Oakley had a famous encounter with a German leader. What happened?

343 Q:

Why did she take the stage name of Oakley?

339 A: As every cowboy moviegoer knows, the Earp brothers and Doc Holliday exchanged gunfire with the outlaw Clanton Gang and the McLaury brothers. For added firepower, Virgil Earp, the sheriff of Tombstone, Arizona, had deputized his brothers Wyatt and Morgan.

340 A: A dentist and a gambler, in that order. John Henry Holliday studied dentistry in Philadelphia before starting a practice in Atlanta. After contracting tuberculosis, he moved to Texas for the weather and soon realized it was more profitable to be a gambler: His coughing spells had made it impossible for him to keep patients.

341 A: Phoebe Anne Moses. Although this daughter of Quaker parents never lived farther west than Ohio, Annie Oakley won well-deserved fame as an expert rifle and shotgun marksman in Buffalo Bill's Wild West show.

342 A: At the request of Wilhelm II, Annie shot the ashes off a cigarette held by the newly crowned kaiser. On her trip, this small-town Midwesterner also performed her tricks for Queen Victoria and several other crowned heads of state.

343 A: The most popular explanation is that she took the name of a neighborhood in Cincinnati, where she and her husband and performing partner lived.

344 Q:
Who invented the Bowie knife?

345 Q:
When did the Black Sox Scandal occur?

346 Q:
Which of the banned players professed his innocence until he died?

347 Q:
The reason behind the team's nickname seems obvious, but there was also a pre-scandal reason for the Chicago team being called the "Black Sox." What was it?

344 A: Alamo fighter Jim Bowie gets all the credit, but it is believed that it was his brother Rezin who invented the famous knife. (In his defense, it was Jim Bowie who popularized it, and both siblings developed their own prototypes.)

345 A: The 1919 World Series. The Chicago White Sox, one of the best teams in baseball's history, were accused of being paid by gamblers to throw the series against the Cincinnati Reds. Though acquitted of charges in court, eight players were permanently banned from playing the game professionally.

346 A: "Shoeless" Joe Jackson. Considered the best player on the team, Jackson's series-high .375 batting average casts doubt on his involvement in the scheme. And his off-the-field records are suspect too: Illiterate and unable to afford his own legal counsel, he was easily persuaded to sign incriminating court documents. Years later, the other implicated players admitted that Shoeless Joe was never at any of the fix meetings with gamblers.

347 A: Their uniforms were generally really filthy. According to a popular story, Sox-owner Charles Comiskey was so cheap that he insisted the players wash their own uniforms. The underpaid athletes refused, and their uniforms became progressively dirtier until they looked almost black. Skinflint Comiskey finally gave in, but he deducted the laundry bill from his players' paychecks.

348 Q:

Who were the victims of the famous Chicago
St. Valentine's Massacre?

1. members of George "Bugs" Moran's gang
2. Fred "Shotgun" Goetz
3. members of Al Capone's gang
4. an optician
5. two off-duty policemen

349 Q:

When was the FBI founded?

1. 1908
2. 1915
3. 1926
4. 1931
5. 1935

350 Q:

How long did J. Edgar Hoover head the FBI and its
predecessors?

1. 29 years
2. 38 years
3. 48 years
4. 51 years
5. 56 years

348 A:
1 and 4. On February 14 (Valentine's Day), 1929, Al Capone's gang members, probably including "Shotgun" Goetz and two men dressed as policemen, lined up seven men against a Clark Street garage wall and gunned them down. Six of the victims were members of the Moran gang; the other was Reinhardt Schwimmer, a young optician who enjoyed hanging out with "real gangsters."

349 A:
1 and 5. The Federal Bureau of Investigation didn't get its name or acronym until 1935, but it was launched as the Bureau of Investigation (BOI) in 1908. The FBI was actually its fourth name, but apparently the only one that stuck.

350 A:
3. Hoover served as the director of the FBI and its precursors for forty-eight years: from 1924 to 1972.

351 Q:

Author J. D. Salinger, actress Marion Davies, and
G-man J. Edgar Hoover had one thing in common.
What was it?

1. an addiction to horse racing
2. they were all born on January 1
3. none of the three ever married
4. they all lived in California

352 Q:

What athlete said, "Hitler didn't snub me—it was FDR
who snubbed me. The president didn't even send me a
telegram"?

353 Q:

Which American track star did not win any medals in
the 1936 Olympics, but was still invited to a personal
meeting with Adolf Hitler because of his "fast finish"?
What prevented him from ever competing again?

354 Q:

Which major-party presidential candidate shot and killed
a young girl when he was only twelve?

351 A:
2. They all began their lives on January 1: J. Edgar Hoover in 1895, Marion Davies in 1897, and J. D. Salinger in 1919.

352 A: Jesse Owens. Even though he won four gold medals in the 1936 Berlin Olympics, the champion sprinter was never invited to the White House by Roosevelt, or for that matter, by his successor, Harry S. Truman. In fact, Owens had to wait until 1955 when President Eisenhower honored him by naming him "Ambassador of Sports."

353 A: Louis Zamperini and World War II. Although regarded as too young to compete at world-class distance running, the "Torrance Tornado" bucked all odds just to qualify for the 5,000-meter event. Tragically, just six years later, Zamperini's B-24 bomber was shot down over the Pacific; after spending forty-seven days on a raft, he was captured by the Japanese and spent the remainder of the war in a POW camp. His brutal imprisonment left him unable to run again, but his incredible story made him a hero.

354 A: Adlai Stevenson was defeated twice by Dwight D. Eisenhower, but his 1952 and 1956 losses probably haunted him less than an incident from his teenage years. In 1912, he unintentionally shot and killed a sixteen-year-old girl. Though absolved of the crime, he never forgot it. Four decades later, he offered searing advice to a woman whose son had accidentally killed another child: "Tell him he must live for two."

355 Q:

"Have you no sense of dignity, sir?" Who spoke these words and to whom were they spoken?

1. Senator William Fulbright to President Richard Nixon
2. Army counsel Joseph Welch to Senator Joseph McCarthy
3. Congressman Preston Brooks to Senator Charles Sumner
4. Jimmy Stewart to a cynical senator in Frank Capra's *Mr. Smith Goes to Washington*
5. President Ronald Reagan to Russian leader Boris Yeltsin

356 Q:

How did the bazooka gun get its name?

357

Q: Seabiscuit was one of the most famed racehorses in the 1930s, but he never won the Triple Crown. Why not?

355 A:

2. With these words, the relatively unknown Welch challenged powerful Senator McCarthy during congressional hearings inspired by the latter's charge of Communist subversion in the American military. These televised interrogations helped cause McCarthy's downfall.

356 A: As unlikely as it sounds, the deadly, armor-piercing, hollow-tube weapon developed during WWII was named after a humorous musical instrument that radio entertainer Bob Burns had whimsically fashioned from two gas pipes and a funnel.

357 A: The three races of the Triple Crown are only open to three-year-old thoroughbreds. Seabiscuit had a rocky start to his career and did not reach his racing potential until he was past the age of eligibility.

358 Q:

What common object did atom bomb–spies Harry Gold and David Greenglass use to confirm each other's identity?

1. similar photographs of a New York landmark
2. a marked copy of an old *LIFE* magazine
3. a Jell-O box
4. matching red scarves
5. creased copies of a subway map

359 Q:

What was the controversy surrounding the naming of the Hoover Dam?

360 Q:

What was the original date for the presidential inauguration and why was it changed to January 20?

358 A:
3. After courier Gold arrived at Greenglass's New Mexico apartment, he announced his presence to the spy with the now-famous code words, "I come from Julius." Then Greenglass retrieved the Jell-O box that Julius Rosenberg had cut in half before he had left New York to work at the Los Alamos laboratory, and the courier and the spy matched their respective halves. Then Greenglass handed over whatever atomic bomb secrets he had stolen.

359 A: The dam was built from 1931 to 1936 and became a symbol of America's ingenuity and resilience during the dark days of the Depression, but it was named for President Hoover, who many blamed for causing the economic disaster. Harold Ickes, FDR's secretary of the interior, insisted on referring to the structure as the "Boulder Dam," even during the dedication ceremony; much his chagrin, the name never took.

360 A: From 1793 to 1933, March 20 was inauguration day. The four-month delay between the election and the inaugural was necessary due to slow travel conditions in the eighteenth and nineteenth centuries. However, in 1933, as the Great Depression worsened and the "lame duck" Hoover administration continued to stall, the late date proved a hindrance to the newly elected Roosevelt, who was ready to take action. The result? The Twentieth Amendment, which changed the terms of office, was ratified before FDR was sworn in.

361 Q:
Why is Giuseppe Zangara more famous for the person he did not shoot rather than the one he did?

362 Q:
How did Douglas "Wrong Way" Corrigan get his nickname and fame?

363 Q:
To what did "Wrong Way" attribute his mistake?

361 A: On February 15, 1933, Zangara mortally wounded Chicago mayor Anton Cermak; however, his real target was president-elect Franklin Delano Roosevelt. The unemployed Italian immigrant fired five shots at FDR's car and struck Cermak accidentally. As he was rushed to the hospital, Cermak whispered to Roosevelt, "I'm glad it was me instead of you."

362 A: On July 17, 1938, pilot Doug Corrigan filed a flight plan at New York's Floyd Bennett Field to fly to California, but twenty-nine hours later, he somehow ended up across the ocean in Dublin, Ireland.

363 A: He claimed that his transatlantic mistake was due to a navigation error caused by heavy cloud cover and low-light conditions, but many believe that his supposed compass misreading was actually a cover for an unauthorized overseas flight. (It is said that he had made several important modifications to his plane, preparing it for a safer transatlantic flight.) In any case, although he lived to be eighty-seven, Corrigan never publicly admitted the ruse.

364 Q:
What happened to Judge Crater?

365 Q:
Who invented Monopoly, the bestselling board game on earth?

366 Q:
What is the Eighteenth Amendment, and how did it complicate millions of Americans' lives?

364 A: No one knows, though not for a lack of hypotheses. On August 6, 1930, New York State Supreme Court justice Joseph F. Crater disappeared. After telling friends that he was attending a Broadway play that evening, he removed papers from his files and cashed a check for a large sum. Late that afternoon, he was seen entering a taxi, but hasn't been seen since. Theories about his disappearance abounded: Was he involved in illegal activities? Was he murdered by someone in the underworld? Did he have a mistress? Was his wife involved with his kidnapping—or worse? Did he run away? In any case, he wasn't officially declared dead until July 1937.

365 A: Charles B. Darrow of Germantown, Pennsylvania, still receives official Hasbro credit as the sole inventor of Monopoly, but recent research has shown persuasively that recognizable variants of the game had already been devised and developed before he supposedly invented it. It was, however, Darrow who took the idea to the bank—and to Parker Brothers—and sold it in 1934. The rest is board game history.

366 A: The amendment, which was adopted in January 1919, prohibited the manufacture, sale, importation, and exportation of intoxicating liquors. Prohibition was repealed by the Twenty-First Amendment, which was adopted on December 5, 1933.

THE UNITED STATES OF TRIVIA

367 Q:
"UNPACK." Who supposedly sent this one-word telegram and to whom?

368 Q:
For what activity is baseball player Moe Berg best known?

369 Q:
Did German combatants ever land in the U.S. during the Second World War?

367 A: According to a popular joke of the time, Democratic candidate Al Smith sent this succinct message to Pope Pius XI after he lost the 1928 presidential election. As the first Catholic standard-bearer of a major party, Smith found himself singled out by those who feared that his victory would mark the beginning of a papist takeover of the country.

368 A: As a player, he was only a journeyman infielder/catcher with a modest .243 lifetime batting average over a sixteen-year career. But as a spy for the U.S. government, Moe Berg was superbly effective. While touring Japan in 1934 with a team that included Babe Ruth, he took photographs of Tokyo that helped guide American bombers during WWII.

369 A: Yes, enemy operatives landed U-boats on New York's Long Island and in Florida. At each location, four German agents were put ashore with instructions to commit "small acts of terrorism [with] incendiary bombs left in luggage depots and Jewish-owned businesses." The project was doomed from the start: The submarine assigned to transport the secret agents ran aground several times. Even worse, all the would-be operatives had landed in the U.S. wearing German uniforms, and the leader of the Long Island contingent actually telephoned FBI director J. Edgar Hoover to confess and betray his cohorts. All were eventually captured.

370 Q:
One famous American poet was a West Point cadet.
Who was he and how did he fare?

371 Q:
When *Leaves of Grass* was first published in 1855,
whose name appeared on the title page?

372 Q:
Early in his career, Samuel Clemens took the nom de
plume "Mark Twain." What does "mark twain" mean?

373 Q:
Ernest Hemingway asserted that all modern American
literature comes from one book. To which novel was
"Papa" Hemingway alluding?

374 Q:
"That's not writing; it's typing" was one famous
American writer's putdown of another's work. Who
was talking about whom?

375 Q:
Jack London, Norman Mailer, Hunter S. Thompson,
Gore Vidal, Upton Sinclair, and James Michener:
What do these writers have in common?

370 A: Edgar Allan Poe's brief stint at the United States Military Academy brought mixed results. In January 1831, after less than seven months there, he was court-martialed and dismissed. However, before he left, Poe convinced more than 130 of his classmates to subsidize the publication of his third book of poetry.

371 A: No one's. Walt Whitman's book might be the most important in the history of American poetry, but its first edition was issued anonymously.

372 A: "Mark twain" is a riverboat term meaning two fathoms deep (which is twelve feet). Former steamboat pilot Clemens took the name, he said, because "it has a richness about it; it was always a pleasant sound for a pilot to hear on a dark night; it meant safe water."

373 A: Mark Twain's incomparable *The Adventures of Huckleberry Finn*, which was first published in the United States in February 1885, two months after its publication in England.

374 A: Truman Capote's flip comment was made about Jack Kerouac's spontaneous prose style.

375 A: They were all bona fide political candidates, though none of them was elected. Sinclair and Vidal came the closest, winning Democratic Party nominations.

376 Q:
In his last acting and directing roles, he called himself "William Goodrich," although his real name would have attracted infinitely more attention. Who was he and why the subterfuge?

377 Q:
Which U.S. president threatened to punch a *Washington Post* music critic?

378 Q:
How old is Mickey Mouse?

379 Q:
When did the first McDonald's open?

1. 1947
2. 1949
3. 1951
4. 1953
5. 1961

376 A: Roscoe "Fatty" Arbuckle was one of the most popular (and well-paid) stars of the silent film era, but he was also at the center of a scandal involving the 1921 death of actress Virginia Rappe that destroyed his career and helped make tabloid newspaper owners rich. Arbuckle was cleared of manslaughter charges after his third trial the following year, but he was nevertheless banned by U.S. film censors.

377 A: President Truman responded to a hostile review of his daughter Margaret's Constitution Hall concert with fighting words. In a handwritten letter, he told critic Paul Hume: "Some day I hope to meet you. When that happens you'll need a new nose, a lot of beefsteak for black eyes, and perhaps a supporter below!"

378 A: Like all other celebrity rodents, Mickey is shy about revealing his age. However, we know that he's past eighty: In fact, Walt Disney always maintains that November 18, 1928, was Mickey's birth date. That's the day that *Steamboat Willie*, the first animated film with sound, debuted at the Colony Theater in New York City.

379 A:
4. The first McDonald's hamburger restaurant opened that year in San Bernardino, California.

380 Q:

How did the chain get its name?

1. Founder Ray Kroc thought the name had a nice American ring.
2. Originally, Kroc believed that he could use the children's song "Old MacDonald Had a Farm" as an advertising gimmick.
3. Nobody knows exactly why Kroc named it McDonald's. In interviews, he gave conflicting accounts.
4. The San Bernardino restaurant was owned by two brothers named McDonald.

381 Q:

Approximately how many hamburgers did McDonald's sell during Ray Kroc's lifetime?

1. 5 billion
2. 10 billion
3. 25 billion
4. 50 billion
5. 100 billion

380 A:

4. Ray Kroc did not own that original hamburger haven, but he did find its business possibilities appetizing. He was fifty-two years old when he convinced brothers "Mac" and Dick McDonald to grant him the first franchises in their concept. Within seven years, the former milkshake-machine salesman was able to buy them out. The rest is burger and fries history.

381 A:

4. By the time owner Kroc died in January 1984, McDonald's had served hungry customers almost fifty billion burgers. It took them only ten years to serve up the next fifty billion.

382 Q:

How did Wendy's get its name?

1. As his first promotion, founder Dave Thomas held a contest to name his first old-fashioned hamburger restaurant. Apparently, the judges liked "Wendy's" best.
2. He gave the eatery his daughter's name.
3. He gave the eatery his daughter's nickname.
4. He named Wendy's after his wife.

383 Q:

When did the United States declare war against Japan?

384 Q:

What is the Einstein-Szilárd letter and to whom was it addressed?

385 Q:

Which of the following scientists did *not* work on the Manhattan Project to develop the atomic bomb?

1. Albert Einstein
2. Edward Teller
3. J. Robert Oppenheimer
4. Enrico Fermi
5. Niels Bohr

382 A:

3. Wendy was the nickname of Thomas's daughter Melinda Lou. When he opened his first Wendy's in Columbus, Ohio, the real Wendy was just eight years old.

383 A: No, it was not on December 7, 1941. President Franklin Delano Roosevelt and Congress made the declaration of war against Japan in the early afternoon of December 8.

384 A: Albert Einstein and Leó Szilárd wrote to President Franklin Delano Roosevelt in August 1939 to inform him of the probability of developing uranium as an energy source to create bombs and to warn him that scientists In Nazi Germany had already begun research on atomic weapons. The letter led FDR to authorize an ambitious U.S. atomic program.

385 A:

1. Einstein was not permitted to work on the Manhattan Project because he was considered a security risk by General Leslie Groves.

386 Q:
What is the Szilárd Petition?

387 Q:
Steven Spielberg's film *Saving Private Ryan* was based
on the true story of which family?

1. Bixby
2. Allison
3. Borgstrom
4. Niland
5. Sullivan

388 Q:
For extra credit, which of the other families also had a
movie made about their war experiences?

386 A: In the summer of 1945, 155 scientists working on the Manhattan Project signed a petition to urge Harry S. Truman, the newly sworn-in president, to not use the A-bomb against Japan. Many of these scientists had agreed to work on the project to prevent Hitler's efforts toward world domination. When Nazi Germany surrendered in May of that year, they felt it morally wrong to use the bomb as an offensive weapon against Japan.

387 A:
4. Set during the Normandy invasion, the 1998 war film was loosely based on the Niland brothers' case. During World War II it was believed that three of the four Nilands were killed in action, leading the U.S. military to search for and return the sole surviving son to American soil. Screenwriter Robert Rodat was inspired when he saw a monument dedicated to brothers killed during the Civil War; he used the Niland story when he transformed the idea into a World War II tale.

388 A: *The Fighting Sullivans* (1944) tells the tale of the five Sullivan brothers who enlisted in the navy with the stipulation that they serve together. All five siblings perished aboard the USS *Juneau* when the ship was torpedoed by a Japanese submarine in December 1942. The Sullivan family's sacrifice became a national rallying cry for the war effort and culminated in a U.S. naval destroyer being named in their honor by President Roosevelt.

389 Q:
The Tuskegee Airmen were a group of African-American pilots during World War II. What was the name given to their First World War counterparts?

390 Q:
What famous woman took a ride with the Tuskegee Airmen in 1941 to help drum up support for the fledgling unit?

391 Q:
What was the code name of the Normandy invasion by the Allied forces on June 6, 1944?

392 Q:
On which Normandy beaches did American military land?

389 A: They had no such counterparts. African-Americans were forbidden to become military aviators during World War I. This policy remained in place until 1939 when federal funds were allocated to train African-American pilots.

390 A: Eleanor Roosevelt. After her flight, she exclaimed, "Well, you can fly all right!"

391 A: Operation Overlord. The cross-channel naval phase was organized under Operation Neptune. "D-Day," the name by which the invasion is known, was used by military planners because the actual date for the landing was subject to final approval.

392 A: Omaha and Utah Beach. The beaches were divided into five designated sectors whose code names are still used today. The British infantry landed at Gold and Sword beaches, and the Canadian forces began their assault at Juno. The most deadly of all the beach landings was at Omaha where American forces sustained thousands of casualties.

393 Q:
What was Operation Husky and who led it?

394 Q:
Despite Patton's success in Sicily, why did Eisenhower select General Bradley to command the U.S. Army in preparation for the invasion of Europe?

395 Q:
U.S. forces had a decisive advantage in the 1942 Battle of Midway because they had broken the Japanese naval code. What was the secret identifier used for Midway?

393 A: Husky was the code name for the 1943 invasion of Sicily. U.S. generals George S. Patton and Omar S. Bradley commanded the land operations alongside British field marshall Bernard Montgomery. The successful invasion inflicted severe casualties on both sides and resulted in the taking of more than 100,000 Italian and German prisoners. Both Patton and Montgomery were eager to claim credit for the military victory: Patton arrived triumphantly in Messina on August 17; Montgomery landed just a few hours later.

394 A: Patton slapped two soldiers who were suffering from battle fatigue. The news made big headlines back home, prompting many politicians to demand his dismissal. Eisenhower believed that Patton was indispensable to the war effort, but that the "slapping incident" demonstrated a lack of discipline that could impact the Normandy planning. Not wanting to take any chances, Eisenhower appointed the less experienced, but more measured general.

395 A: "AF." Unaware that the Americans had broken their code, the Japanese continued to send messages saying that they planned to strike target "AF". By sending a fictitious message, U.S. Navy commanders determined that "AF" signified the Midway Islands, thus telling them the strength, location, and time of the Japanese attack: Forearmed with this precious information, they set up an ambush.

396 Q:
How many naval carriers were lost during Midway?

397 Q:
Of the six men who were photographed raising the flag on Iwo Jima, how many survived the war?

398 Q:
Who took the Iwo Jima photo?

399 Q:
Who was the "Black Dahlia"?

396 A: Five. Four Japanese carriers (*Akagi*, *Kaga*, *Hiryu*, and *Soryu*) were sunk compared to just one American vessel, the USS *Yorktown*. The U.S. also managed to rescue most of its crew, suffering just over 300 casualties, while the Imperial Navy lost ten times as many lives.

397 A: Three. The iconic photograph was taken on February 23, 1945, but the Battle for Iwo Jima raged on for another month. Franklin Sousley, Harlon Block, and Michael Strank were all killed in action. Two surviving marines, Rene Gagnon and Ira Hayes, grew depressed about their combat experiences and bitter about their post-war lives, but navy corpsman John Bradley lived a fruitful life despite his traumatic memories of fighting through one of the most devastating battles of the war.

398 A: Joe Rosenthal, an AP photographer. The image garnered him a Pulitzer Prize and was published on the cover of dozens of newspapers, becoming one of the war's most enduring images.

399 A: Elizabeth Short. Her mutilated body was found in a vacant lot by the Los Angeles police on January 15, 1947. She was given the notorious nickname by the local Hearst newspapers that sensationalized the gruesome murder. The case became one of the most famous unsolved murders in the country, inspiring numerous theories, a bestselling James Ellroy novel, and a successful Brian De Palma film.

400 Q:

Which of the following women were theater stars during the 1890s?

1. Anna Held
2. Edna Wallace Hopper
3. Minnie Ashley
4. Della Fox
5. Florenz Ziegfeld

401 Q:

When Elvis Presley's first single was heard on air, how many times was it played?

402 Q:

Later that night when Elvis did an on-air interview, why did Dewey ask where he went to high school?

403 Q:

Who coined the term "rock and roll"?

1. disc jockey Alan Freed
2. musician Bob Applebaum
3. singer/songwriter Sister Rosetta Tharpe
4. *Billboard* journalist Maurie Orodenker

400 A:
1, 2, 3, and 4. Despite his somewhat confusing first name, Florenz Ziegfeld Jr. was a man, not a woman. He was, in fact, the common-law husband of Anna Held, who earns her place on this list not only for her performing talents, but also for an hourglass figure so pronounced that it engendered rumors she had ribs surgically removed.

401 A: Fourteen. On July 7, 1954, local Memphis DJ Dewey Phillips played "That's All Right" on his popular radio show "Red, Hot & Blue" on WHBQ-AM. The station received so many phone calls that Phillips kept playing the record again and again until the end of his program.

402 A: To let his audience know Elvis's race. Many listeners assumed Elvis was black, but Tennessee was a segregated state, so inquiring about his school was a roundabout way of telling listeners that he was white.

403 A:
4. Fans and musicians had probably been using variants of "rocking and rolling" for years before columnist Orodenker called songs like Tharpe's "Rock Me" "rock-and-roll" in a 1942 *Billboard* piece. By the following year, Merchantville, New Jersey, already had a "Rock and Roll Inn." In the 1950s, disc jockey Alan Freed popularized the music and the term, which had often been previously limited to "race music" by black performers.

404 Q:

What was baseball's "Shot Heard 'round the World"?

405 Q:

What baseball announcer is most associated with calling the home run?

406 Q:

How was the broadcast saved for posterity?

407 Q:

The home-run ball that Thomson hit was never located. What epic American novel chronicles the possible owners of the ball? Hint: Its first chapter is a fictionalized version of the game and broadcast.

408 Q:

Where was the great New York Giants hero Bobby Thomson born?

404 A: New York Giant Bobby Thomson's game-winning home run off Brooklyn Dodgers' pitcher Ralph Branca to win the 1951 National League pennant.

405 A: Russ Hodges. While the game was covered by several television and radio stations, it was Hodges's cry of "THE GIANTS WIN THE PENNANT! THE GIANTS WIN THE PENNANT! THE GIANTS WIN THE PENNANT!" that became the most famous sports broadcast in U.S. history.

406 A: More people heard Gordon McLendon on the national Liberty Radio Network than heard Hodges on the local Giants radio station. However, avid local fan Lawrence Goldberg, who was unable to listen to the game, asked his mother to record the bottom of the ninth inning on his reel-to-reel. Goldberg's tape turned out to be the only recording of Hodges that day, and it has been played over newsreel footage of the game for decades. For many fans, the immediacy and intensity of the call made the game a vibrant memory.

407 A: *Underworld* by Don DeLillo.

408 A: In Glasgow, Scotland.

409 Q:

In the same year that Thomson hit his home run, the U.S. government began extensive testing of atomic weapons. Where were the bulk of their nuclear tests performed?

1. Los Alamos
2. Bikini Islands
3. Marshall Islands
4. Nevada Test Site
5. Salmon Site

410 Q:

Where was the only nuclear test site east of the Mississippi River?

411 Q:

Which of the following writers did *not* testify in front of the House Un-American Activities Committee (HUAC)?

1. Lillian Hellman
2. Dashiell Hammett
3. Clifford Odets
4. Arthur Miller
5. Tennessee Williams

409 A:

4. More than 900 nuclear tests were conducted at the Nevada Test Site. During the 1950s, mushroom clouds could be seen as far away as downtown Las Vegas.

410 A: Salmon Site, located over the Tatum Salt Dome in Mississippi. The U.S. performed two tests there in 1964 and 1966.

411 A:

5. Although he worked with many people called before the committee, Williams himself was never questioned.

412 Q:

Which of the following was a member of the "Hollywood Ten"?

1. Zero Mostel
2. Joseph Losey
3. Ring Lardner, Jr.
4. Martin Ritt
5. Paul Robeson

413 Q:

What event purportedly affected the distribution of the Cold War–thriller *The Manchurian Candidate*?

1. the Bay of Pigs Invasion
2. the assassination of President John F. Kennedy
3. the downfall of Senator Joe McCarthy
4. the Cuban Missile Crisis
5. the publication of photos of the film's star Frank Sinatra with mafia boss Sam Giancana

412 A:
3. While all five were blacklisted by the industry during McCarthyism, only screenwriter Lardner was a member of the original group cited for contempt of Congress after refusing to answer questions from HUAC.

413 A:
2. Released in 1962, the film deals with a Communist plot to assassinate a presidential candidate. Although the studio denied the cause, the film was pulled from theatrical distribution almost immediately after Kennedy's death and remained uncirculated until its 1988 reissue.

414 Q:

How many Communists worked in the Department of Defense, according to the movie *The Manchurian Candidate*? How was the figure derived?

1. 335: based on the estimated number of people black-listed in Hollywood during McCarthyism
2. 140: based on the number of Communist Party members charged under the Smith Act
3. 57: based on Senator Joe McCarthy's original figure in his first speech
4. 57: based on the number of varieties listed on a ketchup bottle
5. 52: based on the number of cards used to play solitaire

415 Q:

Another film, also starring Frank Sinatra, has a connection to the Kennedy assassination. What is the film?

416 Q:

What was the movie that Oswald watched in the Texas Theatre when he was apprehended for shooting JFK?

414 A:

4. The McCarthy-inspired Senator Iselin requests an exact number of Communists to expose during his speech. After eyeing a bottle of Heinz Tomato Ketchup, his wife settles on "fifty-seven card-carrying members of the Communist Party."

415 A: *Suddenly.* In this noir film from 1954, Sinatra plays a ruthless assassin planning to kill the U.S. president when he travels through a small town. It was assumed that Lee Harvey Oswald saw this film on television in October 1963, but he actually saw a different political assassination film, *We Were Strangers.*

416 A: *War Is Hell.* It was part of a double feature that included *Cry of Battle.*

417 Q:
Who else was shot during the assassination of President John F. Kennedy on November 22, 1963?

418 Q:
Almost every adult American has seen the Abraham Zapruder film of John F. Kennedy's assassination. Was it the only photographic record of the 1963 Dallas crime scene?

419 Q:
Lee Harvey Oswald's visits to two countries sparked theories among conspiracy buffs. Where did this restless traveler go and what did he do to arouse suspicion?

420 Q:
In 1948, Harry S. Truman signed a piece of paper that changed the armed forces forever. What was it?

421 Q:
Franklin Delano Roosevelt issued a 1942 executive order that millions of Americans still find disturbing. What was it?

417 A: Texas governor John Connally was seriously wounded while riding with the president and their wives on their way to the Dallas Trade Mart.

418 A: No. In fact, according to Vincent Bugliosi, there were no fewer than thirty-two photographers in and around Dealey Plaza at the time of the shooting. In addition to Zapruder, three other amateur filmmakers recorded at least part of the assassination. However, no other footage can match the vividness of Zapruder's home movie, which was quickly purchased by *LIFE* magazine for $150,000.

419 A: As a teenage marine, Oswald served in Japan and the Philippines, but it was his 1959 defection to the USSR and his brief visit to Mexico only two months before the assassination that have generated controversy. His stay in Russia lasted less than two years, but made this erratic visitor a subject of interest to both Russian and American intelligence; each was worried that he was an agent of the other. His visits to the Cuban and Russian consulates in Mexico City again raised scuttlebutt about his true allegiances.

420 A: His Executive Order 9981 authorized the desegregation of the U.S. armed forces.

421 A: With a one-paragraph statement, FDR authorized the internment of more than 110,000 Japanese-Americans in "War Relocation Camps."

422 Q:
Where did Dwight D. Eisenhower send troops in 1957?

423 Q:
In 1961, what globe-trotting organization was established by John F. Kennedy's Executive Order 10924?

424 Q:
How did Lyndon B. Johnson's 1965 Executive Order 11246 build on civil rights legislation?

425 Q:
Who popularized the expression "A-OK"?

426 Q:
Match the name of the National Aeronautics and Space Administration (NASA) space program with its accomplishment.

1. Viking	a.	first spaceflights for two-man crew
2. Apollo	b.	first humans to land on the moon
3. Mercury	c.	first unmanned satellite
4. Explorer	d.	first man-in-space program
5. Gemini	e.	first spacecraft to land on Mars

422 A: In September, by executive order, he dispatched federal troops to Little Rock, Arkansas, and federalized the Arkansas National Guard to maintain peace during the court-ordered desegregation of U.S. public schools.

423 A: The Peace Corps.

424 A: It established equal employment opportunity for minorities in federal contracts.

425 A: U.S. Air Force lieutenant colonel John "Shorty" Powers. As NASA's public affairs officer during the first manned space flights, Powers used the expression to signify that missions were proceeding as planned. While Powers was known as the voice of the astronauts, he actually borrowed the term from NASA engineers who used it during transmission tests because the "A" sound was easier to hear through static.

426 A:
1 and e.
2 and b.
3 and d.
4 and c.
5 and a.

427 Q:

Who was the first American to travel into space?

1. Neil Armstrong
2. Buzz Aldrin
3. John Glenn
4. Alan Shepard
5. Jim Lovell

428 Q:

What high-intensity experiences during the 1940s helped prepare astronaut John Glenn to become the first American to circle the earth?

429 Q:

Who said, "Houston, we've had a problem."?

430 Q:

Who said, "If I've lost Cronkite, I've lost middle America"?

427 A:
4. On May 5, 1961, NASA launched its first manned space-craft. The mission had been originally scheduled for October of the previous year, but multiple delays meant that Shepard became the second human to enter space, following Soviet cosmonaut Yuri Gagarin just weeks earlier.

428 A: During World War II and the Korean War, this young fight pilot flew—and survived—149 combat missions. For the future U.S. senator, space jaunts were a relatively low-stress activity.

429 A: Jack Swigert, one of three astronauts on the failed *Apollo 13* space mission. In the 1995 movie version of the event, Captain Jim Lovell misquotes Swigert's famous line as "Houston, we have a problem."

430 A: President Lyndon B. Johnson. After Walter Cronkite delivered a televised editorial against the Vietnam War, the beleaguered commander-in-chief responded with these words. Within weeks, he announced that he would not seek reelection.

431 Q:
Lyndon B. Johnson's most famous political ad was aired only once, in 1964. What was it?

432 Q:
Johnson wasn't alone in suggesting that Goldwater was a dangerous politician. Which candidate sent out a pamphlet that read, "Who do you want in the room with the H-bomb button"?

433 Q:
Goldwater was able to defeat his Republican opponent during the California primary because of what happy event?

434 Q:
What was the first dish that Julia Child cooked on television?

431 A: "Daisy Girl." The ad featured a young girl counting petals as she pulls them off a daisy; when she reaches nine an ominous countdown begins, finally cutting to a mushroom cloud explosion. The ad played on fears that opponent Barry Goldwater would use nuclear weapons if elected, and was so controversial that it was immediately pulled. Unfortunately for Goldwater, the ad got plenty of airplay on news programs and talk shows.

432 A: New York governor Nelson Rockefeller. He sent the negative mailing to over two million California voters.

433 A: The birth of Rockefeller's son. Many voters were offended that Rockefeller had left his wife to marry divorcée Margaretta "Happy" Murphy. He was ahead in the polls, but his son's birth three days before the election placed the divorce center stage, putting Goldwater on the moral offensive. Rockefeller dropped out of the race.

434 A: An omelet. When Julia appeared on Boston public television's book program in 1962 to promote *Mastering the Art of French Cooking,* she demonstrated how to make an omelet. The audience response was so enthusiastic that she was offered her own show, *The French Chef*, which became the most popular cooking show on TV.

435 Q:

Which of the following actresses were not born in the United States?

1. Elizabeth Taylor
2. Grace Kelly
3. Audrey Hepburn
4. Natalie Portman
5. Kate Winslet

436 Q:

Which of the following actors were not born in the United States?

1. Cary Grant
2. Yul Brynner
3. Mel Gibson
4. Anthony Quinn
5. Charlie Chaplin

437 Q:

According to the White House projectionist, what is the most requested movie by American presidents?

438 Q:

Which president was the most avid movie fan?

435 A:

1, 3, 4, and 5. Grace Kelly ended up as the princess of Monaco, but was Philadelphia-born and bred. As for the others, Elizabeth Taylor and Kate Winslet saw the first light of day in England; Natalie Portman was born in Jerusalem; and the enchanting Audrey Hepburn was a native of Brussels, Belgium.

436 A:

1, 2, 4, and 5. Mel Gibson has spent much of his career being billed as an Australian actor, but this Peekskill, New York–born star spent his first dozen years in the U.S. of A. Of the others, Cary Grant and Charlie Chaplin spent their early years in their native England; Antonio Rodolfo Quinn Oaxaca (aka Anthony Quinn) was a native Mexican; and Russia-born, future Oscar-winner Yul Brynner was an adult when he first arrived in the U.S.

437 A: *High Noon*, starring Gary Cooper.

438 A: Jimmy Carter. According to White House records, he watched 480 movies during his four years.

439 Q:
Which president was the first to watch an X-rated film in the White House?

440 Q:
What was Lyndon B. Johnson's favorite movie?

441 Q:
What was the first film screened at the White House?

442 Q:
As the controversy surrounding the film grew, Wilson denied any foreknowledge of the movie's content, but what evidence in the film shows that he was fully aware of its racist viewpoints?

433 Q:
What did Wilson reputedly say after seeing the film?

444 Q:
Name the presidents who Forrest Gump meets.

439 A: Also Carter. He watched *Midnight Cowboy* (1969), which is the only X-rated film to win an Academy Award for Best Picture.

440 A: *The President.* This short documentary film about LBJ was commissioned to introduce him to the American people in the wake of Kennedy's assassination.

441 A: *Birth of a Nation.* Woodrow Wilson screened D. W. Griffith's racist epic in 1915.

442 A: To lend academic credibility to his film, Griffith actually quotes passages from Wilson's own writings in *A History of the American People.* In any case, the president made no secret of his racial views: During his administration, he re-segregated Washington, D.C., demoting and terminating numerous African-American federal employees.

433 A: "It's like writing history with lightning." However, many historians claim that it was actually Thomas Dixon Jr. who said this. Dixon was the author of *The Clansman* (the source novel for *Birth of a Nation*) and Wilson's classmate from Johns Hopkins; he had arranged the screening to publicize the movie.

444 A: John F. Kennedy, Lyndon B. Johnson, and Richard Nixon.

445 Q:

During both terms of one U.S. president, a former "significant other" starred in a popular soap opera. Name the White House occupant, his former love, and the TV drama.

446 Q:

Name Barack Obama's three favorite films.

447 Q:

Name the presidential authors of these books:

1. *Six Crises*
2. *At Ease: Stories I Tell to Friends*
3. *Where's the Rest of Me?*
4. *Dreams from My Father*
5. *The Vantage Point*
6. *Decision Points*
7. *A Time to Heal*
8. *The Naval War of 1812*

445 A: In 1981, the year Ronald Reagan became president, his former wife Jane Wyman became the star of *Falcon Crest*, a primetime soap that survived briefly into the administration of her ex-husband's successor. In the series, Wyman played the tyrannical matriarch of the Falcon Crest Winery. In answer to the inevitable question: It's doubtful that President Reagan ever watched the show. In his autobiography, he dismissed Wyman and his eight-year marriage to her in just two sentences.

446 A: In a 2008 interview with Katie Couric, Obama cast his votes for *The Godfather*, *Lawrence of Arabia*, and *Casablanca*.

447 A:
1. Richard Nixon.
2. Dwight D. Eisenhower.
3. Ronald Reagan.
4. Barack Obama.
5. Lyndon B. Johnson.
6. George W. Bush.
7. Gerald Ford.
8. Theodore Roosevelt.

448 Q:

What happened at the famous "Kitchen Debate"?

1. President Dwight D. Eisenhower and Soviet premier Nikita S. Khrushchev argued about the relative merits of their political systems.
2. Vice President Richard Nixon and Khrushchev debated about ideology and the usefulness of household gadgets.
3. President Ronald Reagan and Soviet Communist Party secretary Mikhail Gorbachev sparred about missile defense and freedom of the press.
4. Vice President George H. W. Bush and Gorbachev exchanged opinions about Dolly Parton and cultural values.

449 Q:

Where did the "Kitchen Debate" take place?

1. at a U.S. cultural exhibit in Moscow
2. at a Russian cultural exhibit in Washington, D.C.
3. in a White House kitchen during Khrushchev's first visit to the U.S.
4. in a Kremlin kitchen
5. in a kitchen at Versailles

448 A:

2. Nixon and Khrushchev's impromptu 1959 Cold War exchange of views was the first high-level meeting between U.S. and Soviet leaders since the 1955 Geneva Summit.

449 A:

1. What began as a Nixon-led tour of the exhibit quickly became more spirited as the two leaders wrangled over their nation's accomplishments and future. Much of the debate, which was later televised in both countries, took place in a model kitchen in a typical American home.

450 Q:
Who was the Supreme Allied Commander during
World War II? What was his first post-military job?

451 Q:
"I shall return" was the vow of a famous American
general. Who was he and where was he promising
to return?

452 Q:
In April 1951, Douglas MacArthur was relieved of
all four of his major commands by President Harry
S. Truman. To what did this army general owe his
downfall?

453 Q:
Who chose Richard Nixon as a vice-presidential
nominee?

450 A: Future president Dwight D. Eisenhower. However, before "Ike" took up his White House residence, he served as president of Columbia University.

451 A: General Douglas MacArthur made his much-publicized declaration in 1942, after Japanese troops drove U.S. forces off the Philippine Islands. Two and a half years later, the controversial commander fulfilled his promise.

452 A: The commander-in-chief took this radical action because of MacArthur's increasingly independent communiqués on the ongoing Korean Conflict.

453 A: Believe it or not, it wasn't his future White House boss Dwight D. Eisenhower. A committee headed by Thomas Dewey selected Nixon as the war hero's running mate. Ike later told a news conference that he "basically had no role" in choosing the California congressman as his potential successor.

454 Q:
What was the Checkers speech and how did it get its name?

455 Q:
"If you give me a week, I might think of one. I don't remember." Who said this and why did it haunt one future president?

456 Q:
Which future president skippered a PT boat during the Second World War?

457 Q:
Which future president was the youngest U.S. Navy fighter pilot in World War II?

454 A: In the midst of the 1952 presidential campaign, charges arose that Richard Nixon's backers had raised $18,000 to reimburse him for his out-of-pocket campaign expenses. Such a fund was not illegal, but political pressure forced the future VP to defend himself on national television. His performance was impressive: He emphasized his humble beginnings and frugal lifestyle, bringing the speech to a rhetorical high point with a "confession" that his family had received one gift he refused to return: a little cocker spaniel that his daughter had named Checkers.

455 A: President Eisenhower said this in response to a reporter's request for an example of a major idea of Vice President Richard Nixon's that had been adopted during his administration. It was a throwaway remark at the end of a press conference, but it plagued Nixon throughout his 1960 presidential run.

456 A: Lieutenant, Junior Grade John F. Kennedy commanded the ill-fated *PT-109*, which, just months into his command, was cut in two by an incoming Japanese destroyer. Young Kennedy's brave actions in the aftermath of this tragedy significantly enhanced his charisma after he entered politics. When asked about his heroism, Kennedy assured listeners, "It was involuntary. They sank my boat."

457 A: After becoming a Navy fighter pilot at the age of nineteen, George H. W. Bush flew fifty-eight WWII missions.

458 Q:

After two decades of song and dance musicals in which he usually played an actor/dancer, Fred Astaire took a dramatic role in a movie that captured the mood of its time. What was the film and the issue that it treats?

459 Q:

The Feminine Mystique, Unsafe at Any Speed, In Cold Blood, The Electric Kool-Aid Acid Test, and *The Games People Play.* What do all these very different books have in common?

460 Q:

Where were the Beatles on August 29, 1966?

1. Most of them were in the United Kingdom or elsewhere, but John Lennon was in New York City at the Chelsea Hotel.
2. Paul McCartney was in New York City, being interviewed by David Brinkley.
3. The group was performing in San Francisco.
4. George Harrison was visiting a Buddhist commune in Massachusetts.

461 Q:

When were the first presidential candidate debates? Who won these face-to-face confrontations?

458 A: *On the Beach* was a star-studded 1959 drama about the last survivors of an all-out nuclear war between the United States, its allies, and the Soviet Union. For many people who were anguished over the escalating international arms races of the time, even its final shot of a banner with the words "THERE IS STILL TIME . . . BROTHER" held a poignant message.

459 A: They were all bestsellers during the 1960s.

460 A:
3. On that date, the Beatles played their final formal concert in Candlestick Park. More than two years later, the Fab Four performed together in an informal, largely unpublicized, mostly unseen rooftop concert atop Apple Studios in London. Thus, the San Francisco concert was the last opportunity for fans to really experience the Beatles in their full glory.

461 A: In September and October of 1960, Americans stayed glued to the tube as Senator John F. Kennedy and Vice President Richard Nixon exchanged views in four nationally televised debates. Kennedy's impressive performance in the first debate was regarded by many as the turning point in his winning campaign.

462 Q:
When was the second presidential candidate debate?

463 Q:
When did the United States launch its first satellite?

464 Q:
Who was the first man on the moon?

465 Q:
What were Armstrong's first words when he stood on the moon's surface?

466 Q:
Where is the lunar buggy now?

462 A: Democratic candidates vying for their party's nominations did debate in 1968 and 1972, but it wasn't until 1976 that major party candidates again risked the dangers of a face-to-face televised confrontation.

463 A: The first American satellite was the *Explorer I*, which went into space on January 31, 1958, almost four months after the USSR's *Sputnik*.

464 A: At 10:56 p.m. (EDT) on July 20, 1969, American astronaut Neil Armstrong became the first person to set foot on the moon. Armstrong and Edwin "Buzz" Aldrin left the *Eagle* lunar landing module for more than two hours, during which time they played a little golf and rode around in the lunar buggy. Meanwhile, astronaut Michael Collins orbited the moon in the *Command* module.

465 A: "That's one small step for [a] man, one giant leap for mankind."

466 A: Still on the moon. Fortunately, there is no charge for parking.

467 Q:

Joshua Pusey was one unlucky inventor. What was his problem?

1. On its first demonstration for possible investors, his intricately designed 1901 airplane smashed into a tree, forever grounding his ambitions.
2. Released during the Depression, his board game "Criss-Cross" fell victim to the Scrabble craze.
3. His 1892 innovation of a matchbox turned into an incendiary nightmare.
4. His dreams of an early World Wide Web social network died on the vine because he lacked marketing skills.

468 Q:

The Diamond Match Company, which bought Pusey's inflammatory device, made an even bigger mistake. What was it?

1. It failed to properly patent the matchbox.
2. The company did patent the device, but then made a humane decision that hurt its business.
3. Court cases drained the profits of this former manufacturing titan.
4. Company heads foolishly believed that cigarette lighters posed no threat to their business.

467 A:

3. Pusey's patent for the first book of matches placed the striker on the inside, not the outside of the book. Consequently, would-be smokers often accidentally lit all fifty matches—and sometimes themselves. Not surprisingly, Pusey sold his invention for a meager $4,000.

468 A:

2. In 1910, after President Taft made a public plea to the matchbox behemoth to release their patent for the first non-poisonous match, the company granted the wish of the cigar-smoking chief. The magnanimous grant hurt sales, but thankfully, the Diamond Match Company still exists and prospers.

469 Q:

According to its interpreters, the original *Invasion of the Body Snatchers* was an allegory about what?

470 Q:

On the evening of November 9, 1965, everything changed very suddenly for thirty million Americans and Canadians. What happened?

471 Q:

For how long was 2008 Republican presidential candidate John McCain a prisoner of the North Vietnamese?

472 Q:

The little town of Hollidaysburg, Pennsylvania (population: 5,171), is known for its annual Pumpkin Festivals and Hollidaysburg Hauls, but which of these really qualify as its true claims to fame?

1. Outlaw John Dillinger slept one night there in 1935.
2. The Ant Hill Woods on the town's outskirts teem with underfoot action.
3. The town was the birthplace of gossip columnist Hedda Hopper.
4. It is the birthplace of the Slinky.

469 A: Depending on which cultural critic one reads, this 1956 film was regarded as either a scary portrait of the Communist infiltration of America or a scary indictment of McCarthy brainwashing, but according to production supervisor Walter Mirisch, neither the director, the script-writer, nor the original author saw it as anything other than a thriller, pure and simple.

470 A: All their lights went out. In the Great Northeast Blackout of 1965, electricity shut off without warning in six U.S. states and the province of Ontario. The blackout happened so rapidly and unexpectedly that some radio news shows ignored the unfolding event even as the lights in their own studios were fizzling out.

471 A: His release in March 1973 ended his incarceration of five and a half years.

472 A:
2, 3, and 4 are all true. John Dillinger died in 1934, so in 1935, he was already sleeping with the fishes.

473 Q:

Speaking of Slinkys, how were they invented?

1. A Hollidaysburg merchant saw children "walking" toys down outdoor steps and took the cue.
2. A trash collector salvaging parts of bedsprings recognized that they might have another use and shared the idea with a local handyman.
3. Making experiments with different kinds of wire, a "gadget guy" struck on the idea of a walking toy.
4. An engineer working on a navy project stumbled on the recreational potential of his workday materials.

474 Q:

According to company statistics, approximately how many Slinkys have slunk?

1. 75 million
2. 100 million
3. 200 million
4. 300 million
5. 400 million

475 Q:

Did the U.S. Navy research Frisbees?

473 A:

4. During World War II, Hollidaysburg engineer Richard James was experimenting with anti-vibration devices for a ship's sensitive instruments. When he accidentally knocked some of his test springs off a shelf, he was amused that they "walked," rather than fell. James couldn't sell his brainstorm to the Navy, so he did the next best thing. With help from his wife Betty, he marketed it as a toy. It was first sold at Gimbel's in Philadelphia in 1945.

474 A:

4. The company hit the 300 million mark almost ten years ago, so for Slinkys, the sky seems—paradoxically—to be the limit.

475 A: Yes, they did. In 1968, the Navy spent almost $400,000 on a study of Frisbees in wind tunnels, using cameras and computers. We are not sure about everything that they learned, but we do know that they experimented with Frisbee-like discs, which were molded into battlefield flares to be launched from low-flying aircraft. They also developed a mechanical Frisbee launcher.

476 Q:
What sea mammals has the United States Navy used in recent conflicts?

477 Q:
Who invented the computer mouse?

478 Q:
Until May of 1970, Kent State University was a relatively quiet campus, but all that changed radically within days. What happened?

476 A: During the Vietnam War and the Iraq War, the Navy used bottlenose dolphins and California sea lions for ship and harbor protection and equipment recovery. These intelligent animals were trained to conduct surveillance patrols with a camera held in their mouths, and to work with frogmen to deliver equipment and locate underwater mines and obstacles. Recently, animal-rights advocates have been heartened by reports that these sea mammals will soon be replaced by robotic mine-hunters.

477 A: Among Douglas C. Engelbart's two dozen patents is one for the mysteriously named "X-Y Position Indicator for a Display System," his prototype for the mouse. The device was invented in 1968, but most of us didn't notice Engelbart's brainchild until Apple popularized it in 1984.

478 A: On April 30, President Richard Nixon announced that he was sending troops into Cambodia. By the very next day, demonstrations against the war began on the Ohio campus, as they did throughout the country. Within days, the situation escalated with battles between students and police and the torching of the school's ROTC building.

479 Q:
What happened next at Kent State University that
riveted the nation's attention?

480 Q:
How many times did Muhammad Ali fight Joe Frazier?

479 A: The National Guard had been called to the campus as early as May 2 and had used tear gas against the demonstrators. Two days later, however, matters grew much worse: At a noon rally, twenty-nine guardsmen opened fire on students. In just thirteen seconds, sixty-seven shots were fired, killing four students and wounding nine. Newspapers throughout the country carried front-page stories and photographs of the tragic incident and its aftermath.

480 A: Three. When they met for the first time at Madison Square Garden on March 8, 1971, both were undefeated and had claims to the heavyweight boxing title. In what was called "The Fight of the Century," Frazier defeated Ali by unanimous decision in fifteen rounds. Three years later, Ali won a non-title rematch by decision. In their final meeting, Ali defended his heavyweight championship in the October 1975 "Thrilla in Manila," when the referee stopped the fight in the fourteenth round.

481 Q:
Ali had regained the title from champion George Foreman in 1974. What was Ali's famed technique during that bout?

482 Q:
What happened at the Stonewall Inn on June 28, 1969?

483 Q:
Who owned the Stonewall Inn?

481 A: "Rope-a-dope." After being suspended from boxing for more than three years for refusing the military draft, Ali had to work his way back to a title shot, and he was considered the underdog to the younger and stronger Foreman. In the "Rumble in the Jungle" match held in Kinshasa, Zaire, Ali needed to combat Foreman's dominant strength, so he leaned against the ring's ropes, allowing his opponent to land multiple punches on his body, but not his head. The strategy worked: Foreman's energy was sapped on ineffective jabs, and Ali won by a knockout in the eighth round.

482 A: The New York City police raided this popular gay bar located in Greenwich Village. Hundreds of gay men were routinely entrapped and arrested by vice squads intent on aggressive enforcement of anti-sodomy laws. On this particular night, however, customers resisted, and a riot broke out, resulting in six days of conflict between protestors and police. The event ushered in the start of the gay rights movement.

483 A: The Mafia. "Fat Tony" of the Genovese crime family converted the bar and restaurant into a gay club. Gay establishments were frequently raided by the police, but they were extremely profitable, so the Mafia owned most of the city's gay bars.

484 Q:
A 1970 Greenwich Village townhouse disaster made
international headlines. Why did this local event become
so instantly famous?

485 Q:
After the explosion, two women who later would become
famous were pulled from the rubble. Who were they?

486 Q:
Who were the other notable residents of the townhouse?

487 Q:
In February 1974, a relatively unknown radical group
kidnapped a University of California sophomore at her
Berkeley apartment. What was the group, who was their
victim, and what was their purpose?

484 A: The bomb that prematurely detonated on West 11th Street had been concocted by members of the radical Weather Underground organization, three of whom died in the explosion.

485 A: Kathy Boudin and Cathy Wilkerson. In the pandemonium caused by the disaster, this Weather Underground pair was able to escape and vanish; each soon notched a place on the FBI's Most Wanted list. Wilkerson voluntarily surrendered in 1977; Boudin remained free until her capture after the deadly 1981 Brink's Robbery.

486 A: Merrill Lynch co-founder Charles Merrill and his son, poet James Merrill, had previously lived there. Merrill memorialized the event in a poem entitled "18 West 11th Street." At the time of the blast, actor Dustin Hoffman was a next-door neighbor.

487 A: The self-styled Symbionese Liberation Army (SLA) kidnapped newspaper heiress Patricia Hearst in hopes that this high-profile target could be used as a bargaining chip to gain the release of two imprisoned comrades.

488 Q:
When that unrealistic plan failed, what became their backup demand?

489 Q:
Who encouraged needy Californians to reject the free groceries because "it was aiding and abetting lawlessness"?

490 Q:
Less than two weeks after the kidnapping, the SLA issued the first of several astonishing audio communiqués. What made them so newsworthy?

491 Q:
Where did Bobby Fischer win the World Chess Championship in 1972 and who was his opponent?

492 Q:
On September 20, 1973, two tennis stars played a nationally televised match that was promoted as the "Battle of the Sexes." Who beat whom?

488 A: The SLA had called for $4 million dollars worth of food to be distributed to California's poor. When the prisoner trade fell through, they raised the ransom ante to $400 million. The Hearst family began a food-distribution program, but it was deemed inadequate by the SLA.

489 A: California governor Ronald Reagan.

490 A: On the tapes, Hearst herself could be heard endorsing the kidnappers' demands, denouncing her family, and eventually announcing that she was joining the revolutionaries and taking a new name. She renamed herself Tania, after "Tania the Guerrilla," the girlfriend of Latin-American revolutionary Che Guevara. Before long, she was robbing banks with her former kidnappers.

491 A: In Reykjavik, Iceland, where he beat Boris Spassky in the "Match of the Century." With his victory, Fischer ended twenty-four years of Soviet dominance in the game and became the first American world champion since the nineteenth century.

492 A: Billie Jean King defeated Bobby Riggs in straight sets: 6–4, 6–3, 6–3.

493 Q:
This celebrated match was actually the second tennis
game between the sexes. Who played in the first match?

494 Q: Where and when did the worst nuclear accident
on American soil occur?

495 Q:
What was released just twelve days previous to the
accident to increase public fears of radioactive leakage?

496 Q:
"Yes, we have to say it. Remember this is just a football
game, no matter who wins or loses. An unspeakable
tragedy confirmed to us by ABC News in New York
City." Who said this and what was the event?

497 Q:
How did the FBI come up with code name ABSCAM for
its sting operation against corrupt politicians?

493 A: Just four months earlier, Bobby Riggs beat Margaret Court. Riggs had dismissed women tennis players as so inferior that even a retired champ like him could beat them. King turned down his initial challenge, but Court couldn't resist the fee, believing it was just a harmless exhibition game. However, Riggs's chauvinist posturing was just cover for this cunning strategist; he trained hard before the match and trounced Court. After her loss, King felt the women's game was at risk, so she agreed to play. King won more than respect that day; her fee was $100,000, ten times what Court was paid.

494 A: Three Mile Island plant near Middletown, Pennsylvania, on March 28, 1979.

495 A: *The China Syndrome*, a Hollywood movie about a fictional nuclear catastrophe.

496 A: Howard Cosell announcing on *Monday Night Football* that John Lennon had been shot and killed. In the final seconds of a 1980 football game between the Miami Dolphins and the New England Patriots, Cosell interrupted his normal play-by-play commentary to break the news that the former Beatle was dead.

497 A: It's a contraction of "Abdul Scam." FBI agents posed as the fictional Arab sheik Karim Abdul Rahman and offered bribes to select officials in exchange for political favors. The transactions were all caught on videotape, and over a dozen officials were indicted.

498 Q:

Identify the character who said each of the following quotes in *The Godfather.*

1. "Can you get me off the hook, for old-time's sake?"
2. "I'm gonna make him an offer he can't refuse."
3. "It's a Sicilian message. It means Luca Brasi sleeps with the fishes."
4. "And a man in my position can't afford to be made to look ridiculous."
5. "Leave the gun, take the cannoli."
6. "It's not personal, Sonny. It's strictly business."

499 Q:

Which of these entrepreneur/inventors has or had southpaw leanings?

1. Thomas Edison
2. Bill Gates
3. Robert Fulton
4. Charles Goodyear
5. Steve Jobs

500 Q:

Who said "I'm as mad as hell, and I'm not going to take this anymore"?

498 A:

1. Salvatore Tessio.
2. Vito Corleone.
3. Peter Clemenza.
4. Jack Woltz.
5. Peter Clemenza.
6. Michael Corleone.

499 A:

2. Oprah Winfrey is also left-handed, but as far as we can tell, she hasn't invented anything—yet.

500 A: Howard Beale in the 1976 film *Network*. After being fired by the network for low ratings, news anchorman Beale broadcasts his intention to kill himself on-air. In the film, his anger and lack of "bullshit" make him a ratings hit as he convinces Americans across the nation to fling open their windows and be "mad."

501 Q:

Who delivered the so-called "Malaise Speech" and what were its effects?

502 Q:

Where did the "Miracle on Ice" occur?

503 Q:

The Soviets were so good at hockey that they even beat the North American pros. When the Red Army Team toured the U.S., which was the only NHL team to win?

501 A: In July 1979, President Jimmy Carter delivered his fifth major speech on energy. By this time, the president was worried that Americans weren't listening to his warnings about U.S. overconsumption of energy resources. The tone of this address about a crisis of confidence caused it to be nicknamed the "Malaise Speech," although Carter hadn't used that word. At first, the nationally televised talk seemed to have been a success, but as time wore on, critics began associating it with what they regarded as the president's narrow, pedagogical style.

502 A: Lake Placid, New York. In one of the greatest upsets in sports history, Team U.S.A. defeated the Soviet ice hockey team 4–3 in the 1980 Winter Olympics. Having lost only once in Olympic play since 1960, the Soviets had dominated the sport so completely that it was believed it would take a "miracle" to stop them from winning their fifth straight gold medal. The American team, which consisted mostly of college players, got their miracle and went on to defeat Finland to win the gold.

503 A: The Philadelphia Flyers. During Super Series '76, CSKA Moscow (aka the Red Army Team) was undefeated, having toppled the New York Rangers and Boston Bruins and tied the Montreal Canadiens. In a memorable game in which the battered Soviet team left the ice because of the "Broad Street Bullies'" rough play, the Flyers won convincingly 4–1.

504 Q:
In that same year, why did no Americans compete in the 1980 Summer Olympics?

505 Q:
What was the 1980 "October Surprise" that never was?

506 Q: Who said, "It's kind of hard to sell 'trickle down,' so the supply-side formula was the only way to get a tax policy that was really 'trickle down.' Supply-side is 'trickle-down' theory"?

507 Q:
What was the original name for Pac-Man?

508 Q:
Who were Pac-Man's four enemies?

504 A: The U.S. team boycotted the Moscow-hosted Olympics. President Jimmy Carter led a sixty-five-nation boycott of the event in protest of the Soviet invasion of Afghanistan.

505 A: Republican challenger Ronald Reagan feared rumors that a last-minute deal to free the American hostages held in Iran would help President Jimmy Carter win re-election. When the hostages were released on Reagan's inauguration day, new allegations emerged that Reagan had make a secret deal with the Iranians to hold the hostages until after the election.

506 A: David Stockman. As director of the Office of Management and Budget, Stockman became known for his ferocious slashing of federal programs in the first year of the Reagan administration, as well as for tripling the federal debt during the first term.

507 A: Puck-Man. When Midway licensed the game in 1980 for U.S. distribution, it changed the name to avoid possible vandalism: They thought that changing "P" to "F" would prove too tempting to teenage gamers.

508 A: Blinky, Pinky, Inky, and Clyde. Also known as ghosts or monsters, their respective character names are Shadow, Speedy, Bashful, and Pokey.

509 Q:

What was the first video played on MTV when it premiered on August 1, 1981?

510 Q:

When IBM released its first personal computer in 1981, who was their celebrity spokesman?

511 Q:

When members of the Reagan administration permitted arms to be sold to Iran and the funds to be diverted to Nicaraguan Contras, what domestic laws were they violating?

512 Q:

If there was an international arms embargo against Iran, why were government officials selling weapons to them in the first place?

513 Q:

When the Iran-Contra Affair was exposed, National Security Council staff member Oliver North shredded incriminating documents to cover up the operation. Who helped him?

509 A: "Video Killed the Radio Star" by the Buggles. They never had another hit.

510 A: Charlie Chaplin's Little Tramp. IBM sought to confront its cold corporate image by appropriating the star of Chaplin's most anti-technology movie, *Modern Times*. The advertising campaign was so successful that the Tramp was used as symbol for "Big Blue" for years.

511 A: The Boland Amendment, a group of laws that prohibited the U.S. government from direct funding of the Contra rebels for the purpose of overthrowing the Nicaraguan government. The so-called "Iran-Contra Affair" damaged the Reagan White House.

512 A: To free hostages in Lebanon. Several Americans had been kidnapped and were being held captive by Hezbollah. Iran, desperate for weapons in their war against Iraq, would pressure Hezbollah to free the Americans in exchange for U.S.-made arms. As hostages were released, more were taken, and more weapons requested. As the clandestine operation continued, the profits were funneled to the Contras.

513 A: Fawn Hall. His very comely secretary aided him in a Friday night shredding party. When she testified at the televised hearings in 1987, she became a Washington celebrity.

514 Q:

What was the name of the civilian aboard the space shuttle *Challenger* when it exploded?

515 Q:

Why did Ross Perot withdraw his candidacy for president in July 1992?

516 Q:

Which of the following sites was not shown as part of the opening sequence on *The Sopranos*?

1. Pulaski Skyway
2. Bada Bing! Club
3. Satriale's Pork Store
4. Statue of Liberty
5. World Trade Center

514 A: Christa McAuliffe. She was selected from over 11,000 applicants for NASA's Teacher in Space Project, which was designed to increase public interest in the space program. After training for a year, McAuliffe was killed, along with six other crew members, on January 28, 1986, when the shuttle exploded just seventy-three seconds after takeoff.

515 A: GOP dirty tricks. He claimed that President Bush's campaign was planning to use doctored photographs to spoil his daughter's wedding. Perot refused to offer evidence or identify sources, and the conspiracy-minded tale left his reputation damaged. When he jumped back in the race in October, Perot was unable to regain his early political support.

516 A:
2. While Tony Soprano used the back room of the New Jersey strip club as his office, its exterior was never featured in his drive from Manhattan to his North Caldwell home. The World Trade Center was removed from the opening credits after the attacks of September 11, 2001.

517 Q:

What was the independent record company that released Nirvana's first album?

518 Q:

What is the Palm Beach County "butterfly ballot"?

519 Q:

By how many votes did George Bush win Florida?

517 A: Sub Pop. Beginning in the late eighties, the Seattle-based music label was synonymous with the grunge sound that came out of the Pacific Northwest music scene. In addition to Nirvana's *Bleach*, Sub Pop produced records from Soundgarden, Mudhoney, and a host of others. Not expecting Nirvana's major-label debut record to be a hit, Geffen Records offered Sub Pop a generous royalties deal to buy out the band's contract. When *Nevermind* went on to sell millions of copies, the royalties kept Sub Pop out of bankruptcy.

518 A: A confusing voting ballot used in the 2000 presidential election between George W. Bush and Al Gore. The left side of the ballot lists the Republican candidate first and the Democrat second; however, punching the second hole would cast a vote for Reform-candidate Pat Buchanan, who was listed in the right-hand column. Because this ballot was used only in Palm Beach, and that county had an unusually large number of Buchanan votes (over three thousand) as well as damaged ballots, it was suggested that many people who intended to vote for Gore accidentally voted for Buchanan.

519 A: According to the final certified results, just 537 votes. Bush won the state's twenty-five electoral votes for a total of 271 to win the presidency. Gore won the national popular vote by more than half a million and became the fourth candidate to lose the office by electoral college.

520 Q:

While on the re-election campaign trail in 1992, George H. W. Bush was amazed by what retail technological breakthrough?

521 Q:

Who were the Swift Boat Veterans for Truth?

522 Q:

The combined cost of the 1976 presidential campaigns was $66 million. What is the estimated comparable cost for the 2016 White House run?

523 Q:

"The government has been in bed with the entire telecommunications business since the forties. They have infected everything. They can get into your bank statements, computer files, email, listen to your phone calls." Who spoke these words and to what was he referring?

520 A: At a national grocers convention, the president had his first encounter with an electronic scanner, which had been used in supermarkets since 1976. Apparently, Mrs. Bush did most of the shopping.

521 A: A group of Vietnam War veterans who attacked presidential candidate John Kerry's decorated military record and his later anti-war activities. During the 2004 election, the group wrote a bestselling book and ran a series of television ads claiming that Kerry had misrepresented his service and was "unfit to serve." Even though most of the veterans had never served with Kerry, and their allegations were never substantiated, the attack had an impact on Kerry's November loss. The term "swiftboating" is still used to describe an illegitimate smear campaign.

522 A: Five billion dollars.

523 A: No, it isn't a contemporary activist defending whistleblower Edward Snowden; it is retired NSA agent Edward Lyle (played by Gene Hackman) talking about the agency's ominous powers in the 1998 film *Enemy of the State*. David Marconi wrote the prophetic script.

524 Q:

How many Republican leaders led popularity polls in the two years before Mitt Romney clinched the 2012 nomination for president?

525 Q:

Who said, "Brownie, you're doing a heck of a job," and why did so many people find it inappropriate?

526 Q:

When the Boston Red Sox won the 2004 World Series, they overcame a superstition. What was it and when did it begin?

524 A: Six candidates, according to *Slate*'s aggregation of major surveys from September 2010. In addition to candidate Romney, the former frontrunners were Sarah Palin, Newt Gingrich, Herman Cain, Rick Perry, and Rick Santorum. Now that's a horse race!

525 A: President George W. Bush used these words to praise Federal Emergency Management Agency director Michael C. Brown during the aftermath of Hurricane Katrina. In what was widely perceived as FEMA's incompetent response to one of the country's worst natural disasters, Brown seemed to be doing less than a "heck of a job."

526 A: The Curse of the Bambino. The bad luck began the season after Boston won the 1918 World Series. For reasons that remain opaque, Red Sox owner Harry Frazee sold the team's best player, Babe Ruth, to the New York Yankees. Previously, the Sox had been one of baseball's most successful teams, but after the sale, Boston endured an eighty-six-year championship drought. They did manage to play in four World Series, but lost each in seven-game heartbreaks. And the Yankees? After acquiring the Bambino in 1920, they went on to win twenty-seven titles.

527 Q:
In 2008 Hilary Clinton had lost the Iowa caucus and was predicted to lose the New Hampshire Democratic presidential primary. According to many media sources, what helped her to stage an upset over Barack Obama?

528 Q:
What happened on February 7, 2010, that symbolized the resiliency of New Orleans after so much destruction during Hurricane Katrina?

529 Q:
How many earthlings use mobile devices to access social media sites?

530 Q:
How does Facebook's photograph collection compare with that of the U.S. Library of Congress?

531 Q:
Since its launch in 1977, the *Voyager 1* space probe has traveled 11.6 billion miles into interstellar space and been credited with being one of the most significant scientific projects of all-time. What high-tech software is it carrying?

527 A: She teared up. Initially seen as an unbeatable front-runner, Clinton was just as quickly dismissed as a calculating candidate out of touch with voters. When she seemingly choked up over a friendly question the night before her expected defeat, the media suggested that this humanizing display rallied people to vote for her. Others said it was a contrived cry.

528 A: The New Orleans Saints beat the Indianapolis Colts 31–17 to win the Super Bowl. Less than five years earlier, the Saints' home, the Louisiana Superdome, had been the site where thousands of Katrina evacuees had suffered while the nation watched in horror. When the stadium's damage almost caused the team to leave the city, New Orleans faced yet another setback. Upon returning to the Superdome, the Saints' bold new play led them to their most successful season in franchise history. More importantly, the city embraced their playing style as an emblem of their own rebirth.

529 A: More than 4.2 billion people—and the number is growing. That number includes more than 70 percent of U.S. mobile users.

530 A: With its 140 billion photos, the Facebook archives are more than 10,000 times larger than those of our national library.

531 A: Believe it or not, the *Voyager*'s digital payload has less than 40 KB of memory. That's about 1/240,000th of the memory of a 16GB iPhone 5.